PEOPLES
of
EASTERN ASIA

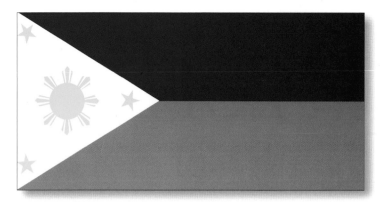

Philippines

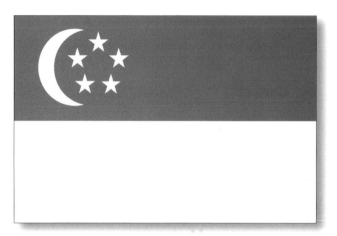

Singapore

Sri Lanka

PEOPLES
of
EASTERN ASIA

Volume 9
Philippines–Sri Lanka

MARSHALL CAVENDISH
NEW YORK • LONDON • SINGAPORE

Marshall Cavendish Corporation
99 White Plains Road
Tarrytown, New York 10591

www.marshallcavendish.com

Consultants:
  Emily K. Bloch, Department of South Asian Languages
    and Civilizations, University of Chicago
  Amy Rossabi, MA in Southeast Asian History
  Morris Rossabi, Professor and Senior Research Scholar,
    Columbia University

Contributing authors:
  Fiona Macdonald
  Gillian Stacey
  Philip Steele

Marshall Cavendish
  Editor: Marian Armstrong
  Editorial Director: Paul Bernabeo
  Production Manager: Michael Esposito

Discovery Books
  Managing Editor: Paul Humphrey
  Project Editor: Kate Taylor
  Design Concept: Ian Winton
  Designer: Barry Dwyer
  Cartographer: Stefan Chabluk
  Picture Researcher: Laura Durman

The publishers would like to thank the following for their permission to reproduce photographs:
  akg-images: 473, 475, 513 (Jean-Louis Nou: 512); Art Directors & Trip (Michael Good: 519, 520; Fiona Nichols: 496; Dave Saunders: 486, 495; Adina Tovy: 481; Peter Treanor: 479, 487); CORBIS: 502, 504 bottom (Dave Bartruff: 500; Ric Ergenbright: cover; Dallas and John Heaton: 491; Dave G. Houser: 507; Hulton-Deutsch Collection: 499; Chris Lisle: 510; Paul A. Souders: 490; Ted Spiegel: 476; Michael S. Yamashita: 498); Eye Ubiquitous (John Dakers: 504 top; Bennett Dean: 492, 494; Laurence Fordyce: 482); Hutchison (Jeremy Horner: 516 bottom); James Davis Travel Photography: 503, 509, 523; David Simson – DASPHOTOGB@aol.com: 477, 478, 483, 516 top, 518; Still Pictures (Henning Christoph: 480; Mark Edwards: 470, 493, 517; Ron Giling: 485, 515, 521; Paul Harrison: 505, 506; Hartmut Schwarzbach: 488 top; Roland Seitre: 488 bottom; Fredrich Stark: 484); Topham/AP: 514.

(cover) A man wears a turban in Rajasthan, India.

Editor's note: Many systems of dating have been used by different cultures throughout history. *Peoples of Eastern Asia* uses B.C.E. (Before Common Era) and C.E. (Common Era) instead of B.C. (Before Christ) and A.D. (Anno Domini, "In the Year of the Lord").

Library of Congress Cataloging-in-Publication Data

Peoples of Eastern Asia.
    p. cm.
  Includes bibliographical references and index.
  Contents: v. 1. Bangladesh-Brunei -- v. 2. Cambodia-China -- v. 3. China-East Timor -- v. 4. India -- v. 5. Indonesia -- v. 6. Japan-Korea, North -- v. 7. Korea, South-Malaysia -- v. 8. Mongolia-Nepal -- v. 9. Philippines-Sri Lanka -- v. 10. Taiwan-Vietnam.
  ISBN 0-7614-7547-8 (set : alk. paper) -- ISBN 0-7614-7548-6 (v. 1 : alk. paper) -- ISBN 0-7614-7549-4 (v. 2 : alk. paper) -- ISBN 0-7614-7550-8 (v. 3 : alk. paper) -- ISBN 0-7614-7551-6 (v. 4 : alk. paper) -- ISBN 0-7614-7552-4 (v. 5 : alk. paper) -- ISBN 0-7614-7553-2 (v. 6 : alk. paper) -- ISBN 0-7614-7554-0 (v. 7 : alk. paper) -- ISBN 0-7614-7555-9 (v. 8 : alk. paper) -- ISBN 0-7614-7556-7 (v. 9 : alk. paper) -- ISBN 0-7614-7557-5 (v. 10 : alk. paper) -- ISBN 0-7614-7558-3 (v. 11 : index vol. : alk. paper)
  1. East Asia. 2. Asia, Southeastern. 3. South Asia. 4. Ethnology--East Asia. 5. Ethnology--Asia, Southeastern. 6. Ethnology--South Asia.

DS511.P457 2004
950--dc22
                                    2003069645

  ISBN 0-7614-7547-8 (set : alk. paper)
  ISBN 0-7614-7556-7 (v. 9 : alk. paper)

Printed in China

09 08 07 06 05 04   6 5 4 3 2 1

Contents

PHILIPPINES

THE PHILIPPINES IS AN ARCHIPELAGO IN THE FAR SOUTHEAST OF ASIA. It contains about 7,100 islands, of which only 880 are inhabited.

Most of the Philippine landscape is mountainous, although there are fertile plains, rolling hills, and narrow valleys on Luzon and Mindanao, and low-lying plains around many island coasts. The highest peak is Mount Apo at 9,690 feet (2,954 meters). Almost all the mountains are of volcanic origin, and twelve are still active. The Philippines lie in an extremely unstable earthquake zone.

Until about 1950, most upland areas were covered by magnificent natural rain forest, but this has been devastated by uncontrolled logging, palm oil plantations, and mining.

Two Filipino friends stand arm in arm. What will their future hold? Their country has many rich resources, but it faces problems of pollution and poverty.

Early History

The first-known inhabitants of the Philippines lived around 30,000 B.C.E. Archaeologists have found stone tools dating from that time, and fragments of human bones dated around 24,000 B.C.E., on the island of Palawan (PAH-luh-wahn). They think that the first inhabitants of the Philippines were Austronesian people. These were the ancestors of the Negrito (nae-GREE-to) people, who still live in rural areas of the Philippines today. The first Filipinos (fih-lih-PEE-noez) survived as nomadic hunters and gatherers in the rain forest, probably traveling in small family groups.

After about 2000 B.C.E., new groups of Austronesian settlers arrived in the Philippines from southwestern China (see CHINA). They traveled to the island of Taiwan (see TAIWAN), and from there sailed in large wooden boats to Luzon (loo-ZAWN) in the northern Philippines. They brought with them seeds of food crops, domesticated animals, and their own skills, including stone tools and pottery.

From their base in Luzon, the Austronesian people soon spread to found new settlements throughout the Philippines. Over the centuries, many of these developed their own customs and their own languages and dialects. Experts think that there are between 87 and 111 different

FACTS AND FIGURES

Official name: *Republic of the Philippines*

Status: *Independent state*

Capital: *Manila*

Major towns: *Quezon City, Davao, Cebu, Caloocan, Zamboanga*

Area: *115,651 square miles (299,536 square kilometers)*

Population: *84,600,000*

Population density: *732 per square mile (282 per square kilometer)*

Peoples: *91.5 percent Christian Malay; 4 percent Muslim Malay; 1.5 percent Chinese; 3 percent other*

Official languages: *Filipino, English*

Currency: *Philippine peso*

National days: *Day of Valor (April 9); Labor Day (May 1); Independence Day (June 12); All Saints' Day (November 1); Rizal Day (December 30)*

Country's name: *Named in 1543 after Prince Philip (later Philip II) of Spain, the former colonial power.*

CLIMATE

The Philippine climate is tropical, with high temperatures year-round, peaking in May and June. There is a rainy season from May to October when flash floods and typhoons are frequent, causing serious damage.

	Manila	Davao
Average January temperature:	77°F (25°C)	81°F (27°C)
Average July temperature:	81°F (27°C)	81°F (27°C)
Average annual precipitation:	79 in. (201 cm)	67 in. (170 cm)

Time line:	First-known inhabitants of the Philippines	Settlers arrive from southwestern China	Chinese and Indians trade with Philippines	Islam arrives in Philippines
	30,000 B.C.E.	2000 B.C.E.	1000 C.E.	ca. 1300–1500

languages or dialects—all closely related to the language of the first settlers—spoken by descendants of these scattered communities in the Philippines today.

These Austronesian people were the ancestors of Malay people, who form the majority of the present-day Philippine population. They lived as farmers. At first they cleared garden plots to grow vegetables and rice by dry cultivation, moving from place to place as the soil became exhausted. They also kept livestock, such as hogs and chickens. Unlike the hunter-gatherers who roamed the rain forests, they settled mainly in lowland areas, where the soil was more fertile. Farming communities were led by *datu* (DAH-too), or chiefs, and divided into different ranks: free families, landless laborers, and slaves, who had mostly been captured in war.

In the first millennium C.E., these farmers learned new skills that enabled them to cultivate more difficult upland terrain, and this tied communities more closely to the same area of ground. New skills included metalworking, irrigation, harnessing water buffalo to pull carts and plows, and growing new varieties of rice in flooded paddies. On the island of Luzon, farmers also cut terraced fields to grow rice on steep, sloping mountainsides.

This useful knowledge was brought by travelers from China and India, and, by about 1000 C.E., fleets from both countries were regularly visiting the Philippines to trade. Indian and Chinese merchants came mostly in search of gold, plus food and water to provision their ships on long voyages. There was also busy local trade among different communities in the Philippine islands and with the states of what are now Malaysia (see MALAYSIA) and Indonesia (see INDONESIA).

Throughout this period, the Philippines remained independent, although local rulers sent tribute to powerful Chinese emperors whose fleets controlled the surrounding seas. Then, between 1300 and 1500, the faith of Islam was brought to the Philippines by Indonesian traders and missionaries. It slowly spread from the southern islands of Mindanao (mihn-dah-NAH-oe) and Jolo (HOE-loe) northward toward Luzon. Muslim missionaries introduced new political ideas, and sultans (Muslim rulers) claimed the right to rule whole islands as overlords. However, most communities continued to be governed by datu, as they had been for many centuries.

For hundreds of years silks, spices, porcelain, gold, and jewels from eastern Asia had been carried to eager customers in Europe and the Middle East by Indian and Arab merchants. They sailed across the Indian Ocean or traveled over land by camel along the silk route from China to the Black Sea. In the late fifteenth century, European explorers began to make daring voyages around the southern tip of Africa and then northeastward toward India. They wanted to take control of the vastly profitable Asian trade—and were also eager to explore the world.

In 1519 Ferdinand Magellan, a Portuguese explorer financed by Spain, sailed from Europe with a fleet of five ships. Like Christopher Columbus before him, he

European explorer Magellan visits Philippines	Spanish soldiers, settlers, and priests reach Philippines	Philippines become center of trade between China, Mexico, and Spain	Filipino people start to rebel against Spain
1521	**1564**	**ca. 1600–1800**	**ca. 1700**

hoped to reach the rich lands of eastern Asia by sailing west, and to claim them for Spain. Magellan's ships made a long, grueling voyage around the southern tip of South America and across the Pacific Ocean, during which many of his sailors died. In March 1521 Magellan landed on the island of Samar (suh-MAHR), in the east of the Philippines. He exchanged gifts with local rulers, tried to convert them to Christianity, and claimed the islands for Spain. He was killed soon afterward in a fight between warring communities on the nearby island of Cebu (sae-BOO).

The Victoria, *sailed by Portuguese explorer Ferdinand Magellan, reached the Philippines in 1521. It was the first ship to sail around the world.*

Spanish Control

In 1564 the Spanish government sent Miguel López de Legazpi to the Philippines. He took 380 men with him, including many Roman Catholic friars (missionary priests). They were ordered to take control of the Philippines, convert the islanders to Christianity, and set up trading links between Spain and rich countries in eastern Asia. After fighting and killing local leaders, they built a Spanish village in Cebu, and declared that the islands were, from now on, to be governed by Spanish law. They also fought against Filipino people who had been converted to Islam, capturing the Muslim city of Maynilad (MAE-nih-lahd), renaming it, and turning it into their own capital city, Manila (muh-NIH-lah).

For the next two hundred years, Manila became the center of a profitable three-way trade, organized by Spanish merchants. They sent Spanish ships to bring silver from Mexico to the Philippines, used the silver to buy silk and porcelain from China, and then shipped the valuable Chinese goods back to Spain. These merchants, together with church leaders, government officials, and army commanders, took control of large areas of land, especially on Luzon, and forced Filipino people to work on them. They also paid for many churches and monasteries to be built, from which missionaries spread the Christian message throughout the Philippine countryside.

Filipino people did not welcome these newcomers, and they bitterly resented the Spanish takeover of their islands. They were angry at the way they were humiliated and forced to obey Spanish colonists. They rebelled many times against Spanish greed and brutality, but

British troops occupy capital of Philippines, Manila	Dr. José Rizal leads rebellion against Spain	Spain declares war on the United States; the United States supports Filipino rebels; Spain hands Philippines to the United States	The United States takes control of the Philippines
1762–1764	1896	1898	1902

Walled City

In 1571 Spanish conquerors made Manila the capital of their new colony. They built fine homes, churches, and government offices there, all in Spanish style. To protect their new city, they surrounded it with a massive wall, 8 feet (2.4 meters) thick and 3 miles (5 kilometers) long. It took more than 150 years to finish building the wall. When complete, it had two forts and a bastion (look-out post), plus 370 gun emplacements. It was guarded by five thousand Spanish soldiers, backed up by ten thousand reserves. Only Spanish people – or their trusted local servants – could enter. Much of this walled city still survives. It is known as the Intramuros (ihn-trah-MYOOR-oes), meaning "inside the walls," district of Manila.

they could not win against well-armed Spanish troops. Filipino people also suffered during the Seven Years' War—a conflict between rival nations in faraway Europe—when British troops occupied Manila from 1762 to 1764. The treaty that ended the war restored Manila to Spain.

By the end of the nineteenth century, Filipino resentment against Spain had reached its boiling point. In 1896 nationalist campaigner Dr. José Rizal demanded independence from Spain. He was captured and executed, but his followers, known as the Propaganda Movement, continued to campaign. They were joined by members of the Katipunan independence organization.

After three years of fighting, in which many Filipino rebels were killed, a truce was arranged. The rebels' leader, Emilio Aguinaldo, went into exile, but demands for independence continued. In 1898 Spain declared war on the United States. Keen to win support from the Filipino people, the United States helped Aguinaldo return from exile. He went on to declare Filipino independence in June that same year. Weeks later, Spain made peace and agreed to hand the Philippines over to the United States.

The Filipino rebels fought the United States from 1899 to 1901, determined to govern their own land, but they were no match for U.S. soldiers, and in 1902 the Philippines came under U.S. control. The United States placed troops, teachers, and missionaries there. With them they brought U.S. culture, and U.S. businesses dominated the Philippine economy.

In 1935 the United States granted the Philippines the right to internal self-government. A new democratic constitution was introduced, and there were free and fair elections to choose a new government. Within six years, however, the Philippines found themselves in the front line of World War II (1939–1945), after Japanese planes bombed the American Pacific Fleet at Pearl Harbor, Hawaii, in 1941. More than a million Filipinos died from hunger, disease, and ill treatment after the islands were occupied by Japan, or they were killed in the fighting between U.S. and Japanese troops in the Philippines.

America gives Filipinos internal self-government	Japanese occupy Philippines in World War II	Philippines becomes independent; Manuel Roxas becomes first president of new Philippine nation	Ferdinand Marcos elected president	Opposition leader Benigno Aquino assassinated
1935	1941–1945	1946	1965	1983

U.S. troops land on the island of Leyte on October 20, 1944, during the battle to recapture the Philippines from Japanese invaders.

Independence

After the war ended, the United States agreed to Philippine independence. In 1946 Manuel Roxas became the first president of the new Philippine nation, but U.S. troops were still stationed on the Philippine islands, and several successive Philippine governments failed to win public support or rebuild the war-torn economy.

In 1965 a new president, Ferdinand Marcos, was elected, promising to make the Philippines "great again," but he faced a grave situation. There was widespread poverty and unemployment. Government ministers, the army, and the police were corrupt, and there was widespread abuse of civil rights. There were terrorist attacks by the communist New Peoples' Army in Luzon, and in the southern islands, a radical Muslim organization, the Moro National Liberation Front (MNLF), demanded a separate Islamic state. In 1972 Marcos declared martial law. This limited freedom further, but it did keep the terrorist movements under some control.

Martial law ended in 1981, when the economy seemed to be improving. Marcos won another term in office that year,

Marcos forced from power; Corazon Aquino becomes president and faces opposition plots	Fidel Ramos elected president of coalition government; arranges truce with Muslim separatists	Economic crisis; Joseph Estrada becomes president
1986	**1992**	**1998**

President Marcos waves to cheering crowds in Manila at his inauguration in 1965. Twenty years later he was forced from office, in disgrace.

threatened by opposition plots. In 1992 Fidel Ramos was elected president in her place. He arranged a coalition with the chief opposition party and a truce with Muslim separatists in the south. Ramos also negotiated with the U.S. government to close its bases in the Philippines. Many Filipinos welcomed this as a sign of independence, although others were unhappy about rights granted to "visiting" U.S. troops by a new deal, signed in 1999.

Facing massive economic problems, Ramos was defeated at the polls in 1998. He was replaced as president by Joseph Estrada, who promised new policies to help the poor, but Estrada—a former movie actor—had little political experience, and by 2001 so many ministers had left his government that the Philippine Supreme Court forced him to resign. He was replaced by his vice-president, Gloria Arroyo. It remains to be seen whether she will be able to solve the Philippines' economic problems, improve human rights, end violence and corruption, and curb the power of some international corporations to damage the Philippine environment.

although the opposition parties were not allowed to campaign in the election. Exiled opposition leader Benigno Aquino refused to be silenced, and he returned to the Philippines to make his views known. Aquino's murder, on Marcos's orders, in 1983 caused worldwide outrage and mass protests in the Philippines.

By 1986 these demonstrations of public anger forced Marcos to resign, and Aquino's widow, Corazon, became president. She was honored as a heroine, but her government was constantly

Like many other countries, the Philippines also faces a growing threat from terrorists. The communist New People's Army frequently attacks Philippine and U.S. government troops, and Muslim separatist group Abu Sayyaf attacks and sometimes kills foreign tourists and Filipino civilians. Abu Sayyaf is also believed to have links with dangerous international organizations, including al-Qaeda.

Vice-President Gloria Arroyo takes over as President; Abu Sayyaf terrorist group kidnaps Americans, killing one.	President Arroyo introduces major financial and administrative reforms	Government signs peace agreement with Moro Islamic Liberation Front (MILF)
2001	**2002**	**2003**

Malay People

The Philippine islands are home to about one hundred different cultural and language groups. Over ninety percent of them are descended from scattered communities of Austronesian farmers who settled throughout the Philippines thousands of years ago. They are closely related to the present-day inhabitants of Malaysia and Indonesia, and are often known as Malays.

Some groups of Malay people living in remote mountain regions still maintain their ancient traditions. Collectively, they are called the *Igarot* (EE-guh-rawt), or mountaineers. Others, such as the Bajau (buhd-JAH-oe), or Badjao, of Mindanao, live close to the sea, as their ancestors have done for centuries. Most Malay people who live in the lowlands follow a modern Westernized lifestyle.

Over the centuries Austronesian men and women married partners from other communities in the Philippines, including Spanish colonists and U.S. servicemen. So today many Filipino Malays have mixed ethnic ancestry. On the whole, this does not cause racial tensions within Filipino

The Bajau people of the southern Philippines live close to the sea. Some are Muslims, but many follow animism (a belief that things in nature have souls).

society; differences of wealth have a much greater impact. There is a vast gap in health, lifestyle, and political power between rich and poor families.

There are, however, political tensions between the majority of the Malay community, who are Christians, and a small minority of Malays (about 4 percent of the total population) who are Muslims. Some Filipino Muslims, who live mostly in the southern islands, are very critical of Philippine government and society and want to set up an independent Islamic state.

As well as Malay people, there are also small communities of Negrito and Chinese peoples living in the Philippines. The Negritos are descended from the earliest inhabitants of the Philippine islands and are related to the indigenous peoples of New Guinea. Ethnic Chinese Filipinos are the descendants of sailors and traders who began arriving from China around 1000 C.E. Unlike the Negrito peoples, whose homes are in mountain rain-forest areas, Chinese families mostly live in big cities and towns, where many have built up successful businesses and professional careers.

Most people in the Philippines wear Western-style clothes, though there is a formal shirt, worn by men, called the *barong tagalog* (buh-RAWNG tuh-GAH-lawg), that is sometimes woven from pineapple fibers.

People stand in line to use the public phones. In big cities Filipino people choose to wear Western-style clothes and make use of modern technology.

Language

The Philippines has two national languages—English and Filipino. English is used by the government and for business and legal dealings; the Philippines is the third-largest English-speaking country in the world. In everyday life, however, Filipino is widely used. It is based on Tagalog, the local language of the region around the capital city, Manila.

Tagalog was spoken by leaders of the fight for independence from Spain. This made it a symbol of national pride, and it became the official language of the Philippines in 1937. It was renamed Filipino to encourage people who spoke other local languages to accept it, but many Filipino people were unwilling to give up their heritage in this way, and today they still speak their own local languages or dialects as well. There are seven major local languages besides Tagalog: Cebuano, Ilocan, Hiligaynon (also called Ilonggo), Bicol, Waray, Pampango, and Pangasinense. All belong to the Malayo-Polynesian language family and are related to Tagalog, but speakers of one cannot understand the others. They use Filipino or English to communicate.

Like many other languages, Filipino has a polite version, used when talking to older, respected people, and an informal version, used among colleagues and friends. People in the Philippines also use two different languages for numbers—Spanish for prices, times, dates, and large quantities, and Filipino for everything else.

In 1990 President Corazon Aquino tried to discourage the use of English as an official language and to promote Filipino. This policy failed, but today some scholars think that a new language, called Taglish (TAHG-lihsh), is developing in the Philippines. Taglish is a mixture of Tagalog and English.

Let's Talk Filipino

Kumusta ho (kuh-MOOS-tuh HOE)	*Hello*
Anong pangalan ninyo? (uh-NAWNG puhng- GAH-luhn NEEN-yoe)	*What is your name?*
Ako si . . . (uh-KOE SEE)	*My name is . . .*
Mawalang-galang na nga ho (muh-WAH-luhng guh- LANG nahng-GAH HOE)	*Excuse me*
Anong oras na? (uh-NAWNG oe-RAHS NAH)	*What time is it?*
Salamat ho (SAH-luh maht HOE)	*Thank you*
Walaa hong anuman (wah-LAAH hawng AH-noo-mahn)	*You're welcome*
Paalam na ho (pah-LAHM nuh HOE)	*Goodbye*

Religion

Christianity is the religion of most Filipinos. The Roman Catholic faith was introduced to the Philippines in the sixteenth century by Spanish settlers and missionaries. Today more than 80 percent of people in the Philippines are Roman Catholics, and about another 10 percent belong to Protestant churches.

Roman Catholics in the Philippines celebrate their faith with many community fiestas, or festivals, honoring local patron (guardian) saints. There are also festivals in honor of the Virgin Mary, to whom Filipino Catholics are especially devoted. All fiestas are joyous occasions—like carnivals. Worshipers dress up in colorful costumes, prepare special food, welcome friends and neighbors into their homes, and sing and dance. There is often a procession, accompanied by musicians, to carry a holy statue through the streets and a special service in the local church. There may also be sports tournaments and even a festival cockfight (an organized fight between two roosters).

Christmas is the most popular fiesta of all. Filipino people celebrate it with a mixture of U.S., European, Philippine, and Chinese traditions. For nine days before December 25, they attend special early-

The Basilica of St. Nino on the island of Cebu. Roman Catholic churches throughout the Philippines are built in European style and decorated with elaborate paintings.

A family from the Ifugao ethnic minority, who live in the mountains of northern Philippines. Their small house is made of local timber and thatch.

singing and ministers who preach in a fervent, emotional style.

Chinese people in the Philippines are mostly Christian, although some families still maintain the traditional Taoist or Buddhist faith of their ancestors. They worship by saying prayers and burning incense at temples. The most famous Taoist temple is close to Cebu City.

morning church services. These are held while it is still dark, so that farmers will not lose any valuable working time. In the Philippines Christmas comes during the harvest season. People decorate their homes with Chinese-style lanterns and sing Western carols. On Christmas Eve almost all families attend Midnight Mass and then return home to a splendid meal. At Epiphany, twelve days after Christmas, they give presents, especially to children.

The Protestant branch of the Christian faith was brought to the Philippines by missionaries traveling with U.S. troops in 1899. Their teachings led to the setting up of more than 350 separate Protestant groups. One of the largest, the Agilpay (Philippine Independent Church), has close links with other Anglican Churches worldwide. Many others belong to an "umbrella" Protestant organization, the National Council of Churches. Most Protestant churches in the Philippines follow a style of worship similar to U.S. gospel services, with rousing hymn

Filipino Muslims

Islam came to the Philippines many centuries ago with the arrival of Muslim traders, around 1300 C.E. Today only a small number (about 4 percent of the population) follow Islam. Most Filipino Muslims live in the south of the country, in Mindanao and Jolo. Like Muslims in neighboring Asian countries, especially Indonesia, many hold a moderate attitude toward their faith, although they are expected to dress modestly, behave with decorum in public, make time for regular prayers, and obey Muslim dietary laws. (This means avoiding pork, shellfish, and alcohol.)

Philippine Muslims celebrate international Islamic festivals, especially *Hari Raya Puasa* (HAH-ree RIE-uh PWAH-sah), which marks the end of Ramadan, the holy month when Muslims fast during the day. This happy time of feasting, visiting, and exchanging presents lasts for three days. At another important festival,

Milod-un-Nabi (MIH-lahd-uhn-NAH-bee), the Prophet Muhammad's birthday, Muslims spend the day more quietly, in prayer and reading the Islamic holy book, the Koran. In August, on the island of Jolo, Muslims commemorate Rajah Baguinda, who brought Islam to their community, with displays of music, arts, and crafts.

Animist Beliefs

In remote country areas, a small number of Malay and Negrito villagers still follow ancient Malay animist beliefs. They believe that everything has a spirit, with the power to help or harm. In particular, these spirits bring fertility to families, animals, and crops. People make offerings to these spirits at important times in their lives, such as setting out on a long journey or

> ### Spirit Carvings
>
> *Woodcarving is a Philippine specialty. For example, the Ifugao (ih-foo-GAH-oe) Malay people, who live in the mountains of Luzon, create* bulol *(boo-LAWL), wooden figures. These portray male and female creator gods, and are designed to keep evil spirits away from stores of food and granaries. Traditionally, each teenage Ifugao boy had to make a pair of these statues before being accepted as an adult. In the past, people said the bulol were so powerful that they could kill rats, ward off thieves, and move around!*

The Ati-Atihan festival, held on the island of Panay, commemorates an agreement made in 1250 between local Ati people and settlers from Borneo.

Pasyon (Easter Festivals)

Easter is the holiest day in the Christian year. For weeks before, worshipers get together to pray and read Bible stories. These meetings, called pabasa *(puh-BAH-suh), often last all night. On Good Friday, groups of volunteers reenact the sufferings of Jesus as he was crucified, often in gruesome detail. Real nails are used to fasten the man playing Jesus to the cross, and he wears a crown of real thorns. This holy drama attracts vast crowds of onlookers, who often get very emotional. Performances are known as* pasyon *(PAHS-yawn), or passion, the word used by Christians in many parts of the world to describe Jesus Christ's death and suffering.*

An actor playing the part of Jesus carries a heavy wooden cross through the streets during the performance of a pasyon at Easter, the most holy Christian festival.

getting married. They also honor the spirits of dead ancestors and pray to them for guidance and protection.

At local festivals, Filipinos celebrate ancient customs, for example tattooing—a traditional sign of courage and high rank among indigenous peoples—with music, dancing, and sports such as bull racing and horse fighting (where two stallions fight each other in a ring, watched by spectators).

Family and Society

Families play a vitally important role in the lives of most Filipino people. Many, especially older people, rely on their families for their survival. Traditionally, families are large, and even today many Filipino women have three or four children. Family life provides love, companionship, help, a sense of belonging, and often also food, money, sympathy, and shelter to other family members in difficulties. There are few state welfare benefits in the Philippines. Filipino parents work hard and go without things they want in order to provide their children with healthy food and a good education. In return, children are expected to care for their parents in illness and old age.

Life for many Filipino people is hard. Yet many visitors to the Philippines are impressed by the gracious and generous spirit shown by the men and women they meet. Filipino children are taught good manners and to have respect for older people at an early age. They also learn to control their own feelings, treat other people with calmness and gentleness, and not to make public displays of anger, affection, or other private emotions (except at religious occasions). All this helps them fit in more easily and usefully as members of their family or community group.

Filipinos work hard to rebuild many Philippine cities in the latest architectural styles, using modern materials such as concrete, steel, and glass.

Women's Lives

Unlike women in many other Asian countries, those in the Philippines play a full part in public life and hold many top positions in arts and sciences, politics, and the professions. There have been two women presidents, Corazon Aquino and Gloria Arroyo, and there are many women senators and judges. Women have equal civil and legal rights with men. They can vote, own property, get an education, and train for any career.

However, women are also expected to fulfill their traditional roles as wives and supporters of men, mothers of children, homemakers, and hostesses. Women from ordinary families rely on mothers, sisters, and other family members to help them cope, but wealthy women employ many female servants. This has led to accusations

Community Values

Filipino people value hospitality; bahanihan *(buy-YAH-nih-han), or cooperation; courage; hard work; and determination. They have a special phrase for the bond between people who give and receive help —* utan na loob *(oo-TAHN-uh-loob), meaning "debt of honor." There is also a special term,* bahala na *(ba-HAH-luh NAH), to describe the way Filipino people cope with poverty and misfortune. It means "all things must pass — so get on with life, try your best, and enjoy things if you can."*

high-rise offices and hotels and glamorous shopping malls. There are museums, art galleries, theaters, and government offices, and exclusive residential districts where a small, very wealthy minority live in elegant, air-conditioned mansions surrounded by high walls and beautiful gardens. Most city dwellers, however, occupy crowded apartment buildings in busy streets, where the air is often polluted with traffic fumes. About one-fourth of Manila's residents have no proper home, but live as squatters in makeshift shelters with no clean water or sanitation.

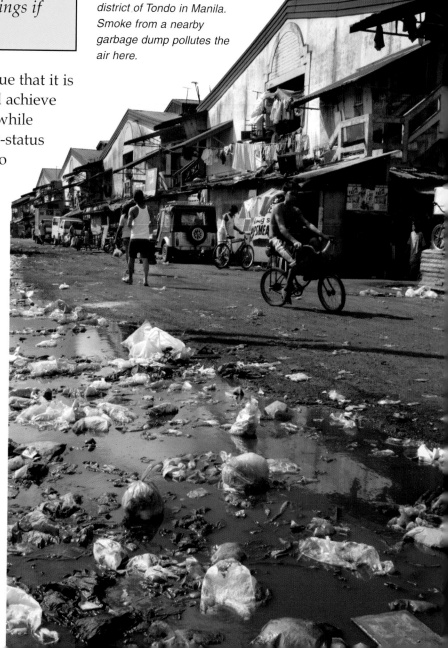

Trash litters the streets in the slum district of Tondo in Manila. Smoke from a nearby garbage dump pollutes the air here.

of exploitation. Some people argue that it is not fair that a few women should achieve fame, power, wealth, and praise while relying on other poorly paid, low-status women to run their homes and do their chores for them.

Living in Cities

Since independence in 1946, Philippine cities have been growing fast, especially Manila, the capital, and its surroundings. Known as Metro Manila, this region has seen its population increasing by 4 percent per year. Filipino people leave their homes in the country and move to cities in the hope of improving their lives. Hoping to find work and earn enough to feed and house their families, sadly, many are disappointed.

Manila and other big cities, such as Cebu, have dynamic modern business districts, with

Living in the Countryside

Away from the big cities, about 60 percent of the Filipino people live in villages or country towns. In the Tagalog language these are called *barangays* (BAH-ruhn-GAEZ), meaning boats. Historians think the name survives from the time, many hundreds of years ago, when Malay people arrived to settle in the Philippines. Each boatload of migrants formed the core of a new community, and members

Local fresh fruit and vegetables, including red onions, lychees, and limes, for sale in a Philippine market. Many fruits, especially pineapples, are also grown for export.

Barangay Laws

Each barangay, or village community, has its own laws, passed down by word of mouth from generation to generation. New laws are made by the datu, or leader, of each community. They were traditionally announced to the people living there by a "town crier" who shouted them out in the streets. He also announced the penalties in this way, which could be unusual. In one law code, made in 1433, minor crimes, such as singing when people were sleeping or cheating in business deals, were punished by exposure to ants or being made to swim for hours!

However, this tradition is weakening, partly because of Americanization of Philippine society after World War II, because of modern international media such as satellite TV, and also because so many people, especially young workers and students, are moving to towns, leaving their traditions behind them.

relied on each other to survive. This feeling of cooperation still survives today.

A typical village might have two hundred households, grouped into separate neighborhoods. It might also have a Roman Catholic church, an elementary school, and one or two small stores. Traditionally, many neighborhoods were occupied by related families, who felt close ties to each other and to their hometown as a whole. Even today, neighbors in the countryside are expected to help one another with major projects, like building or repairing houses and clearing new farmland, and with everyday tasks like sharing tools or preparing food.

Larger villages have many more facilities, such as markets, which farmers travel to once a week to sell fresh products; a larger church; a high school; several different stores; a rice-threshing plant; a corn mill; and a pit for cockfights.

There might also be a theater, a clinic or small hospital, a bank, a hotel, fine houses owned by local landowners, and smaller, but still comfortable, homes for middle-class residents such as doctors, teachers, and lawyers. These larger homes, particularly if they were built before 1900, will probably be in ornate Spanish-colonial style, as will most Catholic churches. Protestant churches are often built in dramatic modern designs and may have very tall spires.

Most ordinary families live in simple one- or two-story houses made of materials such as wood, bamboo, and thatch, or more modern homes made of concrete, with roofs of sheet iron. Around the coasts of southern islands there are still some stilt-houses built along the shore, raised high above the water on tall wooden poles.

In remote areas few villages have electricity or running water. Wealthier families can afford oil-powered generators, and neighborhoods share communal water pumps. In the rest of the countryside, however, most homes have electric power,

a flush toilet, and at least one cold-water faucet. Most families also have a television set, although they may not have a telephone. The Philippine telephone system is notoriously unreliable.

Agriculture

The Philippines' hot, rainy climate and fertile volcanic soils mean that crops grow well and ripen quickly. Rice is planted on terraces cut in the steep mountain slopes; corn and coconuts, other chief crops, are grown on lowland around the coast. Philippine farmers also grow sugarcane, bananas, sweet potatoes, cassava (a tropical plant with edible roots), tobacco, and coffee. They raise water buffalo (to pull plows and carts), goats, hogs, chickens, and ducks for meat, and keep dairy cattle.

Farming plays an important part in the Philippine economy, providing jobs for four out of every ten workers, but it contributes only 15 percent of the national income, and shortage of land is a problem. Before 1900 most of the Philippines were covered in

Filipino children in the countryside. Most Filipino families are large—with at least three or four children—and very close knit. Relatives often work together on farms.

Banaue Rice Terraces

These spectacular "steps," cut into the steep mountainside 4,000 feet (1,200 meters) above sea level in the north of the island of Luzon, were created more than two thousand years ago. They were made by the Ifugao people to grow rice, and they feature a remarkable network of bamboo pipes and mud-walled channels — one of the earliest artificial irrigation systems in the world. In 1994 the Banaue (buh-NOW-ae) terraces were declared a World Heritage Site, but they are still in danger. They are threatened by earthworms, which burrow into the soil, creating tunnels that weaken the terrace structure, tourism, which interrupts water supplies, and by changes in farming techniques. Ifugao farmers can no longer afford to farm the terraces using traditional varieties of rice, for which they were designed. It is cheaper and easier for them to plant modern crops elsewhere.

These spectacular terraces at Banaue, on the island of Luzon, were cut into the hillsides for growing rice more than two thousand years ago. They are still in use today.

dense natural rain forest. Only the lowland areas were intensively used for farming. The soil there was more suitable and less likely than mountain land to be washed away by heavy rains or sudden floods. In mountain regions local communities cleared small areas of rain forest for garden plots or built terraces in carefully chosen areas of hillside.

Traditionally, Filipino land was worked as small family farms, though the Spanish colonists farmed large estates, worked by landless laborers. Today there are millions of farm workers who still own no land and have to find work where they can. They are among the poorest people in Filipino society. In the twentieth century the old ways of farming came increasingly under threat from logging and mining companies, and from large agribusiness enterprises. In 1998, for example, 100,000 families were moved from their farms on Mindanao to make room for oil-palm plantations.

Harvesting sugarcane on Negros Island in south-central Philippines. The canes will be crushed to extract the juice, which will be boiled and crystallized in huge refineries.

which they sold. In the late twentieth century, large areas of coastal mangrove swamp were cleared to set up fish and shrimp farms. At first these were productive, but other fishers found that by removing the mangroves, the fish farmers had destroyed the habitat where many wild sea creatures lived, and their catches declined. Local craftworkers found that other useful plants, such as the abaca, which provided fiber used to make mats, baskets, and furniture, had also been destroyed.

The Philippines' fishing industry has also suffered from climate change, which has brought many more storms and floods, which pollute the fishing grounds with

Pressure on farmland also came from the fast-growing population. As the number of Filipino families increased, so did the need for food, but rapidly expanding cities and towns also took over land that had once been used for farming. As a result, thousands of lowland farming families were forced to leave their land and move to the cities or migrate to upland regions, where more land was available.

Fishing

Around the coast many Filipino families have traditionally made a living from catching fish and other seafood. They have also dived under water to gather pearls, corals, and beautiful tropical seashells,

A diver returns to the surface with a shell to sell to tourists. Uncontrolled fishing and shell collecting are damaging the Philippines' coastal environment.

chemicals from the land. The use of cyanide by Filipino fishers—as a quick and easy way of catching fish by stunning them—has also led to dangerous pollution.

Economy

The Philippines has a mixed economy. About 40 percent of the population works in farming or on plantations; around 20 percent for the civil service or other state concerns, such as education; roughly 18 percent in service industries, such as catering and tourism; about 10 percent in manufacturing; and around 6 percent in construction. The remaining workers have a variety of jobs, from traditional craftwork to deep-sea diving.

The most important Philippine industries include textiles, pharmaceuticals, chemicals, automobile assembly, petroleum refining, logging, and the processing of agricultural products such as oil palm and sugarcane. Most are based in Manila, but new industrial sites were developed on Cebu, Negros (NAE-groez), and Mindanao in the late twentieth century. New microelectronics enterprises, making use of Philippine workers' high standard of education, were also set up, and the former U.S. military base at Subic (SOO-bihk) Bay was transformed into a free-trade zone. Other new factories were set up to make garments for multinational companies and furniture from rain-forest products such as bamboo and rattan (tropical rain-forest creepers). These have frequently been criticized for paying low wages. It is also alleged that the furniture factories use illegally felled rain-forest timber.

The Philippines is rich in natural resources, with deposits of copper, cobalt, chromite, nickel, silver, gold, and iron, and also asphalt, gypsum, sulfur, coal, and oil. There are also quarries of limestone and marble. Increasingly, mining and quarrying has raised concerns for the environment.

In 1998 the Philippine economy faced serious problems as a result of the Asian financial crisis. Export sales fell, prices and profits were reduced, unemployment increased, and production slowed. Poor weather conditions also led to a major fall in agricultural production. The economy has recovered to some extent since then, but government polices have led to a growing burden of debt. The government owes a vast sum to banks and other investors, equal to about a whole year's output from the Philippine economy. Recently, ministers have announced plans to reorganize the economy, privatize many government services, and reform the tax system.

Filipinos Overseas

Because of unemployment and poverty at home, many Filipinos seek work overseas. Often they are well educated and well qualified, and sometimes manage to find professional jobs that give them the chance to make full use of their skills. More often, however, they have to take low-status jobs, as laborers, domestic servants, store assistants, or nannies. In wealthy countries, such as Saudi Arabia and the United States, the wages they earn in these low-ranking jobs are far more than they might earn at home. So they remain abroad, away from their homes and families, and send money back to their parents, spouses, or children to help them lead better lives.

Food and Drink

Philippine food reflects the nation's diverse history and multicultural heritage. It is a mixture of local Malay dishes with styles of cooking introduced by Chinese traders, Spanish colonial rulers, and U.S. armed forces. It has also borrowed ingredients and techniques from neighboring Thailand, Japan, Korea, and Vietnam.

Favorite Philippine foods are hearty, and strongly flavored. Main meals feature generous quantities of meat and fish. Typical dishes are *lechon* (lae-CHAWN: roast suckling hog), *adobo* (uh-DOE-boe: chicken or pork with garlic and vinegar), and *menudo* (mae-NOO-doe: stewed liver), all of which have Spanish origins. Another favorite Spanish dish is *arroz caldo* (ah-ROEZ CAHL-doe), a thick rice soup with chicken, garlic, ginger, and onions. Local meat dishes include *kare-kare* (KAH-reh KAH-reh: tripe and oxtail) and, in the north of the island of Luzon, *aso* (AH-so), which is dog.

Fish and other seafood may be served freshly caught, grilled, or baked with stuffing—this is called *bangus* (BAHN-guhs). Alternatively it may be thinly sliced, sprinkled with spices, lemon juice, or vinegar, and served raw. Seafood such as mussels are steamed and served with ginger and green leaves; cuttlefish is cooked with coconut milk and vinegar. Tiny salted shrimps called *bagoong* (buh-GOONG) are mixed with tomato, eggplant, and onions. These shrimp also form part of a popular dish called *pancit* (PAHN-siht)—noodles with chopped meat and vegetables in a salty, shrimp-flavored sauce.

Vegetables are often cooked in meat dishes rather than served separately to accompany other dishes. Beans and bean sprouts, bitter melon, onion, peppers, sweet potatoes, ramie leaves (like spinach), tomatoes, cassava, and squash are some

Shoppers stop for a drink, light refreshment, or a meal in the food court of a shopping mall at Iloilo, on the island of Panay.

of the popular foods served in Filipino meat dishes.

Filipinos like to share meals with friends or meet to eat in large family groups. So they serve several dishes at once, along with freshly boiled rice, for diners to help themselves to what they want. This means that dishes often cool down before everyone has a chance to sample them, but many Filipino diners prefer their food warm rather than piping hot. Traditionally, food was served on banana leaves and eaten with the fingers of the right hand. There are still some specialty restaurants that continue

Chopped fish, served raw with lemon juice or vinegar, is a Filipino favorite. The acid in the juice or vinegar makes the fish appear cooked.

Adobo

This popular Philippine stew has a rich, savory flavor. It can be made with any lean meat. Philippine cooks choose chicken or pork. Serve with boiled rice and chopped onions.

You will need:

> *2 onions, peeled and chopped*
> *1 lb (500 grams) lean meat, cut into*
> *   1-inch (3-cm) cubes*
> *2–3 cloves garlic, peeled and chopped*
> *2 tbsp (30 milliliters) cooking oil*
> *3 tbsp (45 milliliters) vinegar*
> *4 tbsp (60 milliliters) soy sauce*
> *2 tsp (10 milliliters) sugar*
> *1 cup (250 milliliters) water*
> *black pepper to taste*

Fry onions gently in oil until soft. Add meat and fry, stirring, until lightly browned. Add all other ingredients. Cover and simmer until meat is cooked—about 30 to 40 minutes. Add more water if necessary to make sure pan does not boil dry.

This quantity serves four people.

---

this custom, but in most homes Western-style silverware and dishes are used.

At parties guests may be offered *pulutan* (POO-loo-tahn), or little dishes, to eat before the main meal is served. Afterward there is usually fresh fruit for dessert. The Philippines' tropical climate means that many delicious fruits grow there and can be bought in street markets year-round. They include pineapples, bananas, limes, custard apples, durians (a foul-smelling but delicious fruit), carambola, melons, and, the Filipinos say, the sweetest mangoes in the world.

On special occasions meals might end with Malay desserts such as *halo-halo*—mixed fruits with crushed ice, sweetened beans, and condensed milk—or Spanish-style favorites, such as *leche* (LAE-chee) flan, which is a caramel cream, or *brazos* (BRAH-zoes), meringue stuffed with egg custard, but these sweet treats are more often eaten

491

as snacks. The Philippines' warm climate means that many people spend their leisure time outdoors, pausing from time to time for a light, tasty bite to eat.

As well as sweet snacks, there are also many savory ones, including *tapa* (TAH-puh: dried beef with onion rings), *pata* (PAH-tuh: crispy fried hog skin), and *lumpia* (LOOM-pee-uh: Chinese-style spring rolls, filled with chopped vegetables or ground meat and served with peanut sauce). In the late twentieth century, many international fast-food companies opened restaurants in towns and cities throughout the Philippines, serving Western-style burgers, ribs, and chicken to diners in a hurry.

Members of the Chinese community often drink tea, but, for other Filipinos, the favorite beverage is coffee, served with milk and sugar or, after meals, taken black. For something more refreshing, Filipinos drink *buko* (BOO-koe: coconut juice), *guyanbano* (gie-uh-BAH-noe: soursop juice), or tea made from a miniature lemon, known as *calamansi* (cah-luh-MAHN-see). Soda and other carbonated beverages are also popular.

The best-known brand of Filipino beer (San Miguel) is sold throughout much of eastern Asia and is very cheap to buy in the Philippines. Local distilleries also make their own versions of vodka, whiskey, gin, and rum. Away from big cities, families brew traditional *basi* (BAH-see: sugarcane wine) and *tuba* (TOO-buh: palm wine). As Christians, most Filipinos have no objections to drinking alcohol, although members of the Muslim community avoid it.

Health and Education

A baby boy born in the Philippines today can expect to live until he is sixty-six years old, and a baby girl until she is seventy-two years old, but these overall figures conceal a wide gap in health and life expectancy between the very rich and the very poor.

Wealthy families can afford to pay for a healthy standard of living, with spacious modern homes in clean surroundings, good food, and expert medical care. There

A Filipino woman displays both traditional and modern medicines at her market stall in Manila, the Philippines' capital city.

Students travel home from school, literally piled on top of a bus. Most of the best schools and colleges are in cities and towns, a long way from many students' homes.

are many private hospitals and clinics in big cities and towns. Poor families, especially in cities, live in cramped, unhealthy homes, without modern sanitation and in polluted environments. They cannot afford a healthy diet or professional health care. Instead, they rely on traditional remedies or visit clinics run by charities and churches. There are also some state-run hospitals, but they are poorly equipped.

Poor families cannot afford to protect their children against dangerous diseases, such as diphtheria, polio, and cholera, which are carried by polluted water and spread fast in crowded slums. Stray dogs and cats, which scavenge for food, carry deadly rabies in cities; many bats in caves in the countryside are also infected. Rural rivers, lakes, and paddies are home to parasitic worms and water snails. Mosquitoes spread malaria, and lice carry typhus. There are also a growing number of people infected with HIV and AIDS.

The Philippine education system is modeled on that of the United States, and all lessons are taught in English. There are thousands of public and private, fee-paying schools and 162 colleges. The most prestigious schools are in Manila, where over two million young students live. In the late twentieth century, new institutions, such as the Asian School of Management, were set up in Manila to train graduate students for top careers in the expanding economy of eastern Asia.

Private pupils begin nursery school at about three or four years old; for other children (the majority), public schooling starts two years later. All pupils receive six years of elementary education (from six to twelve years old), followed by four years at junior high school. Many then leave, but others stay on until they are eighteen, to

Fighting Cockerels

The traditional sport of cockfighting is still very popular with Filipino men, especially in country towns and villages. Owners take great care of their birds, giving them special foods and herbal medicines. They also take pride in each bird's appearance, washing its feathers with special shampoo to make them shine. Before a fight, owners fasten long, sharp spikes onto each bird's legs. It uses these to attack its opponent. The loser of the cockfight usually dies, and even the winner is often injured. Owners and spectators all bet large sums of money on the results.

A fighting cock with its owner before the start of a fight. This traditional sport has been criticized for its cruelty, but it is still popular.

prepare for college, where courses last from four to six years.

The school year begins in June and ends in March. At college, the year is divided into two semesters, from June to October and November to March.

Most Filipino people value education and are keen to graduate. In the country as a whole, more than 94 percent of adult men and women can read and write. This percentage is higher in big cities and lower in remote country districts. There, many students leave school before they are sixteen to try and find work to help support their families.

Art, Entertainment, and Sports

Many regions of the Philippines are famous for their own local crafts. Specialties include baskets made from rattan, plus handwoven fabrics from northern Luzon and southern Mindanao, shell craft from Cebu, bamboo furniture from central Luzon, and silver jewelry from Baguio (bah-GWEE-oe).

In complete contrast, artists living in Philippine cities have developed expert skills and use the most modern techniques to create animated movies and comics. Many Hollywood movie companies send work to Philippine studios, and Philippine comic books have a cult following throughout Asia and the United States.

Music and dance also play an important part in Philippine cultural life. Traditional music is still very popular, especially soulful *kundiman* (KOON-dee-mahn) songs and haunting tunes played on the *kulintan* (KOO-lihn-tahn), a collection of gongs, and the *kutyapi* (koot-YAH-pee), a two-stringed lute. Filipino audiences also enjoy Western-style music, especially when performed by Filipino superstar Lea Salonga, who chants songs from hit musicals. Crooner Julio Iglesias Jr., whose mother is from the Philippines, is very popular, and folk singer Freddy Aguilar, whose songs protest against injustice, has many fans.

Young Filipinos listen to international rock groups, on radio, television, and CDs, and go to concerts by local bands. Heavy metal is a favorite musical style, and Japanese-style karaoke is very popular among friends, families, and colleagues enjoying an evening out at a café or bar.

There are many dance groups dedicated to preserving traditional dances, such as the *tinikling* (tih-NIH-klihng), from the Visayan (vuh-SIE-uhn) Islands. Like many other Filipino dances, it was inspired by nature—dancers hop over bamboo poles, mimicking the light, graceful movements of birds. There are also many Filipino ballet dancers who have trained to perform in Western style and have found starring roles with companies in the United States, Europe, and Russia.

Basketball was brought to the Philippines by teachers from the United States and is now the most popular sport. Highly-paid professional players compete in leagues sponsored by top businesses. The most successful stars become national heroes. Another very popular sport, jai alai (HIE LIE), came to the Philippines from Spain. It is based on the ancient Basque game of pelota (pae-LOE-tuh), and it is similar to modern-day squash. Players use curved wicker bats to hurl a hard ball against a wall. Their opponents then have to hit it. Fast and furious matches are played by teams of six, and Filipino spectators like to bet on the results.

A basketball match on the island of Camiguin, in the southern Philippines. Teams play in national leagues sponsored by big companies and have many loyal fans.

495

SINGAPORE

THE NATION OF SINGAPORE LIES OFF THE SOUTHERN TIP OF THE MALAY PENINSULA. It consists of a main island, also called Singapore, plus about sixty smaller islands.

Singapore is separated from Malaysia, to the north, by the Johor Strait and from Indonesia, to the south, by the Strait of Malacca and the Strait of Singapore. It is linked to Malaysia by a causeway. New land has been reclaimed from the sea around the coast.

The islands of Singapore are mostly flat and low, with a few small cliffs along the coast and shallow river valleys inland. The natural vegetation is tropical rain forest, but more than 95 percent of the land is built on or cultivated.

A young girl from Singapore's Chinese community, dressed up for a festival parade. More than 70 percent of Singaporeans are of Chinese ethnic heritage.

CLIMATE

Singapore has a hot, very humid, tropical climate with heavy rainfall year-round. During the northeast monsoon, from December to March, the rains often cause floods. During the southwest monsoon, from June to September, there are violent squalls of wind and rain, called Sumatras.

Average January temperature: 79°F (26°C)

Average July temperature: 81°F (27°C)

Average annual precipitation: 92 in. (234 cm)

History

Singapore (SIHNG-uh-poer) was first settled by groups of nomadic hunter-gatherers around 50,000 B.C.E. By 2000 B.C.E. new groups of settlers had arrived, probably from southwestern China. They were the ancestors of the Malay (MAE-lae) people, who now live in Malaysia and Indonesia, as well as in Singapore.

From 100 C.E. traders from India and China visited the Malay Peninsula to buy tin and gold. They passed close by Singapore, and may have landed there to trade in valuable tropical woods. During the next twelve hundred years Singapore was ruled by several different Southeast Asian kingdoms, including the Srivijaya (sree-wih-JAW-yuh) Empire, based on Sumatra, and the Majapahit (mah-huh-PAH-hiht) Empire, based on Java (both now part of Indonesia). According to ancient chronicles, the city of Singapore was founded during this era—in 1299.

Around 1400 C.E. Singapore became part of the powerful Melaka (muh-LAK-uh) Empire, based in the far southwest of the Malay Peninsula. The rulers of Melaka controlled the valuable trade in spices that were produced on nearby islands and sold for high prices to traders from Europe and the Middle East. After about 1500, European merchants tried to take control of this trade for themselves, and in 1511 Portuguese sailors and traders conquered Melaka. The old rulers of Melaka escaped, and set up a new kingdom in Johor (juh-HOER), at the southern tip of the Malay Peninsula.

In 1819 British merchants, led by Sir Thomas Stamford Raffles, set up a new trading base on the island of Singapore. They aimed to control warships, passenger ships, and cargo ships sailing from Europe to colonies in India and the Far East—and to weaken their great rivals, the Dutch.

In 1826 the British united Singapore and the island of Penang (off the northwest Malay Peninsula) with Melaka, to form the British Straits Settlements, governed from British colonial headquarters in India. Singapore was made a crown colony in 1867, ruled directly by the British government in London.

FACTS AND FIGURES

Official name: *Republic of Singapore*

Status: *Independent state*

Capital: *Singapore*

Major towns: *Jurong, Bedok, Seletar*

Area: *225 square miles (583 square kilometers)*

Population: *4,500,000*

Population density: *20,000 per square mile (7,719 per square kilometer)*

Peoples: *77 percent Chinese; 14 percent Malay; 8 percent Indian; one percent other*

Official languages: *Malay, Chinese, Tamil, English*

Currency: *Singapore dollar*

National day: *Independence Day (August 9)*

Country's name: *Singapore is named after the city of Singapore, which means "Lion City."*

Time line:	First inhabitants, nomadic hunter-gatherers, arrive in Singapore	Ancestors of Malay people arrive from southwest China	Traders from India and China visit the Malay Peninsula to trade	Island of Singapore ruled by Srivijaya and Majapahit empires
	ca. 50,000 B.C.E.	**2000 B.C.E.**	**100 C.E.**	**100–1300**

Sir Thomas Stamford Raffles (1781–1826)

Remembered today as the founder of colonial Singapore, Raffles was born on a ship near Jamaica. He joined the British East India Company, which controlled the very profitable trade between Britain, the Indian subcontinent, and Southeast Asia. In 1811 he was made the Company's senior officer and was based on the island of Java (now part of Indonesia). Between 1818 and 1823 he moved to take charge of the nearby island of Sumatra. During that time he persuaded the Company to take control of Singapore and turn it into a thriving port. He encouraged thousands of Chinese workers to migrate there, made ambitious plans to rebuild the city in Western style, opposed slavery, studied tropical plants and animals, encouraged education for Malay people, and promoted free trade.

A statue of Sir Thomas Stamford Raffles, remembered as the man who colonized Singapore for the British in the early nineteenth century, stands in Empress Place.

Under British rule, Singapore grew rapidly. Ships from many nations docked at its harbor, and merchants from many lands brought and sold the valuable goods they carried there. Thousands of workers from India and China migrated to Singapore, to work as longshoremen, laborers, sailors, builders, porters, and storekeepers.

A small minority of well-educated Singaporeans—mostly Malays—shared in this prosperity, but many local people remained poor. They lived in crowded, unhealthy slums and often went hungry. Many became addicted to the drug opium. These tensions helped create support for communist political parties in China—

Singapore region ruled by Melaka	Portuguese conquer Melaka	British unite Singapore, Penang, and Melaka to form British Straits Settlements	Singapore made a crown colony; British develop docks and international trade	Japanese invade Singapore	Talks about independence held in London
ca. 1400	**1511**	**1826**	**1867**	**1941**	**1956–1958**

where many Singaporeans had originated—as well as in Singapore. The communists criticized conditions in Singapore and also supported Chinese communists who fought fiercely against growing Japanese power.

Japanese troops invaded Singapore in 1941. They renamed the island Shonan (shoe-NAHN: Light of the South) and treated the local people brutally. Singaporeans from all communities welcomed British soldiers when they returned after Japan's defeat at the end of World War II, in 1945, but they did not want a return of British colonial rule. The communists organized strikes and large demonstrations, and new political parties were formed, all calling for independence.

From 1956 to 1958 talks to discuss self-rule for Singapore were held in London. Singapore was given the right to govern itself, but defense and foreign policy was still controlled by Britain. In 1959 the most powerful new political party, the People's Action Party, led by Lee Kuan Yew, won a landslide victory in the general election and called for complete independence, as well as a merger with neighboring Malaya. Their plans won public support in a second vote in 1962.

Faced with this democratic mandate, Great Britain agreed. In 1963 Singapore, Malaya, and Sabah (SAW-buh) and Sarawak (SA-ruh-wak)—both on the island of Borneo—joined together to form the independent nation of Malaysia. However, this arrangement did not last long.

Lawyer and independence campaigner, Lee Kuan Yew, became the first prime minister of independent Singapore in 1959 and remained in control of the nation until 1990.

Singapore quarreled with Malaya over their plans to give preferential treatment to ethnic Malays, and in 1965 Singapore broke away to become the independent nation of Singapore.

With independence, the government of Singapore faced a huge challenge. The first prime minister, Lee Kuan Yew, and his colleagues decided that rapid modernization, new technology, and economic development held most promise for the future. They also expected Singaporeans to give up some of their

People's Action Party wins elections and demands independence	Singapore becomes independent as part of Malaysia	Singapore breaks away from Malaysia to become an independent nation	Lee Kuan Yew retires; new governments continue his policies of modernization and economic and social policies
1959 and 1962	**1963**	**1965**	**1990**

Lion Dancers celebrate Chinese New Year. Dressed in lion costumes, they parade through the streets, accompanied by drums and cymbals, to ask for blessings from the gods.

political rights and freedoms to create a community that was well educated, hardworking, law abiding, self-disciplined, and deeply patriotic.

Within ten years, Singapore had become one of the most prosperous countries in the world. Lee Kuan Yew retired as Prime Minister in 1990, but governments that followed him continued with similar economic and social policies. Singapore's strong economy helped it survive the financial crises of the late 1990s, and today it faces the future with ambitious plans for new technology and even greater prosperity.

Peoples of Singapore

Singapore is one of the most densely settled countries in the world. It is home to people of several different ethnic origins. The Singapore government encourages them to develop a shared Singaporean identity, based on moral values and economic prosperity, but also to celebrate their own traditional cultures, customs, and festivals.

Malays and indigenous peoples make up 14 percent of Singapore's population. In official statistics they are not listed separately. By the year 2000 there were very few indigenous people left in Singapore, and their traditional lifestyle and rain-forest homeland had almost completely disappeared.

The Malay community is large, numbering about half a million people.

Government launches new plans to develop businesses that depend less on export markets; SARS epidemic causes widespread concern	Government signs Defense and Security Agreement with the United States
2002–2003	**2003**

A few Malays still follow their traditional way of life, surviving by fishing and farming, but the majority work alongside other peoples of Singapore in places such as high-tech factories, offices, hospitals, and schools.

The Chinese

The Chinese are the largest group in Singapore, making up more than 75 percent of the population. The earliest Chinese settlers were merchants who had settled at the trading port of Melaka from around 1500 C.E. Some Chinese men married Malay women already living in Singapore, and their descendants became known as *Perankan*, meaning "Straits Chinese." They followed a combination of Chinese and Malay traditions, speaking their own Malay dialect, wearing Malay clothes, but following Chinese social customs and religious practices.

After 1821, settlers came directly to Singapore from many different parts of mainland China. At first these Chinese migrants worked as farmers, laborers, and craftspeople. They built homes and set up communities where they could speak their own local dialects and maintain local traditions.

Today, people of Chinese ancestry hold many of the top jobs in Singapore's government and business communities. A few old regional "Chinatown" communities still survive, but many Chinese people now live in modern apartment buildings beside fellow Singaporeans.

Other Settlers

The second largest group of settlers in Singapore came from the Indian subcontinent. Like the Chinese settlers, the first Indians traveled to Singapore from the Malay Peninsula around five hundred years ago. They were mostly soldiers and traders. Later, in the nineteenth century, Indians were brought to Singapore by their British rulers, to be laborers, or migrated to seek work as clerks, teachers, storekeepers, and money lenders. Most Indians came from southern India, but a few families originated in northwestern India, Bengal, and Sri Lanka.

Merchants from Arabia also came to Singapore to trade. Like Europeans, who traveled there to manage shipping businesses and rubber plantations while the British ruled the Malay Peninsula, a few decided to settle permanently. These Arabs and Europeans often married local Malay people. Their descendants, of mixed ethnic ancestry, still live in Singapore today.

In the late twentieth century, U.S. and European expatriates with special skills, for example, in computing or finance, arrived in Singapore to live and work. Some were excited by the challenge of developing new businesses based on modern technologies. Others hoped to make their fortunes in Singapore's fast-growing, free-market economy.

Language

To reflect the nation's multicultural identity, Singapore has four official languages: Malay (spoken in Malaysia, and very similar to the language of Indonesia), Chinese, Tamil (a language from southern India), and English. Malay is the national language, but English is used by the government and administration.

Most Singapore citizens speak at least two languages—their own traditional language, plus English. In the past, people who came to Singapore from different regions of China all spoke their own dialects and often could not understand one another, but recently the Singapore government introduced a "Speak Mandarin" campaign, encouraging Chinese people to speak this standard form of Chinese so that they can all communicate clearly with each other.

Religion

People from different ethnic backgrounds in Singapore all follow their own faiths, but there is little hostility or discrimination on religious grounds. Religious toleration is official government policy, and, to help achieve this, all religious education is banned in schools.

Most Chinese people in Singapore respect the ideas and follow patterns of worship taken from three ancient Chinese traditions—Confucianism, Buddhism, and Taoism. They consult fortune-tellers and practitioners of feng shui (FEHNG SHWEE), a system that studies the relationship between people and the environment in which they live. They also honor ancestor spirits, especially at the Ching Ming festival, when families traditionally visit tombs to ask their ancestors for guidance and protection.

Indian families in Singapore are mostly Hindus. They worship many different gods and visit beautifully decorated shrines. They celebrate many traditional festivals, especially *Deepavali* (dee-puh-VAH-lee), the festival of lights that commemorates the victory of Lord Krishna over the evil Narakasura, symbolizing the victory of good over evil. Another important festival

The Sri Mariamma Temple (founded in 1827; rebuilt in 1862) is the oldest Hindu temple in Singapore. It is decorated with carvings of Hindu gods and spirits in southern Indian style.

is *Thimith* (TIH-mihth), when worshipers walk barefoot over burning coals to show their devotion to the gods.

Members of Singapore's Malay community are mostly Muslims and have a moderate attitude toward their faith. They wear modern, but modest, clothes and often work on Friday, the traditional Muslim holy day. However, they do celebrate important Muslim festivals, such as *Hari Raya Puasa* (HAH-ree RIE-yuh PWAH-sah) at the end of the month of Ramadan. As a sign of respect for the faith of Islam, these are national holidays for everyone in Singapore.

Society

Since independence, the lives of Singaporeans have been shaped by the government's own beliefs about society, often described as "Asian values." These are based on the ancient Chinese philosophy of Confucianism, established by the great philosopher Kongfuzi (551–479 B.C.E.), known in the West as Confucius, which encourages respect for elders, obedience to authority, striving for success, personal humility, and loyalty to family and community.

The Singapore government does not admire Western-style democracy and criticizes some Western societies for being immoral, lazy, and complacent. It argues that citizens should be responsible for their own health, welfare, and prosperity, and should also be willing to give up personal freedoms to benefit society as a whole.

Critics of the Singaporean government argue that these "Asian Values" are

Good Behavior

Singapore has some of the toughest laws in the world, and a very active police force to make sure that they are obeyed. Smoking in public places, dropping litter, jaywalking, and failing to flush public lavatories are all punished by heavy fines. Vandalism is punished by caning (a punishment beating with a cane) and imprisonment. Bringing drugs into the country is punishable by death.

dangerously authoritarian and limit free speech. They claim that many Singapore citizens have become "*kiasu*" (kee-YAH-soo)—that is, pushy, competitive, and obsessed with success. Critics say that strict government laws are antidemocratic

Dressed in fashionable Western-style clothes, Singaporeans stroll through the streets of their city's quiet old riverside district, with its many fine restaurants.

The inhabitants of these modern high-rise buildings, built by the government, have hung the Singapore flag from almost every balcony as a sign of national pride.

and deny workers and political dissidents their human rights; they also complain that rapid industrial development has ruined Singapore's historic heritage and its natural environment.

In many ways these criticisms are true. However, the government's policy has been very successful. Singapore is a safe and comfortable place to live. Public services, including health and education, are good, and there are clean streets, tempting stores and restaurants, efficient transportation services, and many open spaces and entertainment complexes where people go to spend their leisure time.

The government provides well-built homes for almost all Singaporeans. More than 86 percent of Singaporian families live in modern houses and high-rise apartment buildings built by the state-run Housing Development Board and sold or rented to them at subsidized rates. All these homes have clean drinking water, gas, and electricity. More than half of all Singaporean households can also afford air conditioning and own a personal computer.

The Singapore government also prides itself on providing a safe environment. The crime rate is low, and falling. Although Singapore is a big, crowded city, it is free from litter and vandalism. The fact that many people take pride in their country and want to share in its development and prosperity may also play a big part.

Bright city lights reveal the dramatic skyline of Singapore's new Boat Quay district, with its tall office buildings, hotels, and shopping malls.

Economy

Since independence in 1965, Singapore has become one of the wealthiest countries in the world. It has been transformed from a poor country, with an unskilled workforce, to a developed industrial economy with many highly educated, well-trained workers. This is due to the determined hard work of its people, the high quality of the schools and colleges, and government economic policies designed to develop business opportunities. Singapore's position on international shipping routes has also helped its harbor to grow and many related businesses, such as ship repairing, petroleum refining, and manufacturing deep-sea oil-drilling equipment, to develop.

In the early years after independence, government policies were designed to increase Singapore's wealth by making sure that all its workers could find a job and earn enough money to support their families. There are few state benefits, but the government compels all workers and all employers to contribute to compulsory health insurance and pension plans.

By declaring its support for free enterprise, low taxes, and unregulated

The Port of Singapore

The island of Singapore lies at the meeting point of international shipping routes that have been important for almost two thousand years. Today more than four hundred shipping companies are based there, and the port of Singapore is the busiest in the world – with almost 150,000 vessels visiting every year. It is Asia's main transshipment hub, where goods, packed in massive containers, are off-loaded from one cargo ship to another. It also has a glamorous passenger terminal, where cruise ships can anchor. It is the world's top bunkering port (a harbor where oil is stored) and the third-largest oil-refining center.

Singapore's national symbol, the magical merlion *(half fish, half lion)*, watches over the entrance to the city's huge harbor.

trade, the government encouraged foreign companies to set up businesses in Singapore. It sited factories close to large housing developments, where workers lived, and passed strict labor laws that allowed companies to limit workers' rights — for example, the opportunity to strike — so as to maximize their profits.

Singapore has very little land and few natural resources. Because of this, its government decided to develop businesses based on high-value skills, such as engineering and electronics, and processing food, beverages, oil, and rubber. Building, transportation, and communications industries also grew quickly.

The government encouraged new information-based industries, such as computing and financial services, and biotechnology and life-sciences companies. It expected workers to take part in lifelong learning programs, to improve their skills and increase their productivity.

The tourist industry is also a major employer in Singapore. Almost eight million people visit the country every year. Visitors come to admire Singapore's striking mixture of old and new buildings, its traditional city districts, such as Chinatown and Little India, to go shopping in its magnificent air-conditioned malls, and to see the wonderful collections of rare orchids and tropical birds in its famous parks.

Food

Many tourists visit Singapore to enjoy expertly cooked, delicious food. There are many fine restaurants and hotels all over the island, serving food prepared in Chinese, Indian, Malay, or Western styles, but most Singaporean families cook meals at home or buy take-out foods from the thousands of food stalls that line Singapore's city streets. Whichever way it is cooked, all Singaporean food makes use of fresh ingredients — fish caught from local

Fresh vegetables for sale in one of Singapore's many street markets include carrots, melons, beans, Chinese cabbage, and ginger root.

seas, pork and chicken from local farms, and rice, fruit, and vegetables imported from nearby Malaysia and Indonesia.

Favorite Chinese dishes include *nasi ayam hainan* (nuh-SEE ah-YAHM hie-NAHN: rice cooked in chicken broth served with sliced, steamed chicken and ginger-chili sauce), *chye tow kueh* (CHEE-yeh TOW koo-EH: a fried cake made of grated white radish, eggs, and spring onions), *bak kut the* (BAHK koot-TAE: pork ribs with soy sauce, herbs, and ginger), and *char siew pow* (CHAHR-soo-POW: steamed bun stuffed with pork in a sweet sauce). Dishes made with rice or wheat noodles are also very common. *Foochow* (foo-CHOW) noodles are steamed and served with oyster sauce, dried fish, and spring onions. *Hokkien* (hoe-KYEHN) fried noodles are cooked with prawns, pork, and vegetables in a rich sauce.

The most popular Indian meals include fish-head curry (red snapper heads with okra and tomatoes in a spicy sauce), *biryani* (buhr-YAH-nee: saffron rice with vegetables and chicken or fish), and *murtabak* (muhr-TAH-bahk: thin sheets of dough wrapped around minced mutton, then grilled). Many Indian people are Hindus, and therefore do not eat beef.

Malay dishes are often served with *ikan bilis* (EEK-ahn BEE-lihs: crispy fried anchovies) and *sambal* (sahm-BAHL: toasted spices mixed with salt). Malaysian *satay* are tiny cubes of grilled meat or chicken, served with spiced peanut sauce. *Tahu goreng* (tah-HOO guh-REHNG) is fried soybean curd with bean sprouts, and *rendang* (rehn-DANG) is spiced beef stew in coconut sauce. However, the most widely eaten

Chinese sausages, flavored with hot spices, for sale in Singapore. The city's cooks import the best ingredients from many Asian lands to prepare delicious meals.

Malay dishes are *nasi campur* (NAH-see KAHM-poor: boiled rice served with a selection of spicy meat or vegetables) and *mee goreng* (MEE goe-REHNG: fried egg noodles with chilies and spices). Most Malay men and women are Muslims, and therefore do not eat pork or shellfish.

For dessert, people from all communities in Singapore eat fruit—usually cool and fresh, but occasionally dipped in batter and fried, or mixed with jelly, syrup, and condensed milk. There are many delicious tropical fruits available, including mangoes, bananas, passion fruit, guava, *longgan* (LAWN-gahn: like lychee), and papaya.

Tea and coffee are favorite beverages. Chinese people prefer their tea weak, served without milk or sugar, but most people from other communities take their tea strong, with plenty of both. Milk, sugar, and sometimes spices are also added to coffee. Fruit juice and soft drinks are very popular in Singapore's tropical climate.

Fried Rice Noodles

You will need:

35 oz (1 kilogram) fresh rice noodles or 12 oz (340 grams) dried rice noodles

5 tbsp (75 milliliters) cooking oil

2 onions, peeled and chopped

5 oz (150 grams) cooked meat (pork is popular) chopped into thin strips

3 cloves garlic, peeled and chopped

2 red chilies, chopped (remove the seeds for a milder taste)

3 sticks celery, cleaned and chopped, or half a small cucumber, peeled and cut into thin strips

7 oz (200 grams) bean sprouts

6 spring onions, washed and chopped

1 tsp (5 milliliters) sesame oil (optional)

4 tbsp (60 milliliters) soy sauce

If using fresh rice noodles, rinse in boiling water. If using dried rice noodles, cook according to directions on packet.

Heat 2 tablespoons of oil in a saucepan or wok. Add onions and cook until they are soft and pale brown. Stir from time to time. Add meat, garlic, chili, and celery or cucumber. Cook over high heat for three minutes, stirring frequently. Add bean sprouts and spring onions, and cook for about three more minutes, stirring frequently. Remove cooked mixture from heat. Set to one side, and keep it warm.

Heat 3 more tablespoons of oil in large deep frying pan or wok. Add noodles. Stir and cook gently until noodles are hot. Add cooked mixture, sesame oil, and soy sauce. Stir again. Keep on cooking until whole dish is hot.

This quantity serves four people as a light meal.

Many Malays are Muslims, and therefore do not drink alcohol, but Chinese and Indian people like to drink locally made brandy or Singapore's own Tiger-brand beer. Stylish hotels serve cocktails such as the well-known Singapore Sling—a mixture of gin, fruit juice, and cherry brandy, which was first served in British colonial times.

Health Care

Singapore's high standard of living is matched by good health care. Treatment in hospitals and doctors' clinics is provided by the government and by private health insurance plans. Patients are expected to contribute to the cost of their treatment. Fees depend on income; for the poorest people, treatment is free.

The government also runs many health education and public welfare projects, for example, to warn against smoking and promote exercise. It also provides a school dentist service, immunizes children against dangerous infections, and screens older people to detect chronic diseases such diabetes or high blood pressure. As a result of these medical services, together with good food, a high standard of housing, and clean water supplies, a young girl in Singapore can expect to live until she is eighty-three years old, and a young boy until he is seventy-seven—two of the longest life expectancies in the world.

Around two-thirds of all deaths in Singapore are caused by diseases of old age, especially heart disease and cancer. The rest are chiefly a result of accidents and tropical infections such as malaria, which is carried by mosquitoes.

In the future, care for elderly people is expected to become one of Singapore's main medical needs, as individuals live longer and the whole population grows older.

Education

Education in Singapore is designed with a double purpose, to help individual students develop their natural abilities and learn new knowledge and skills, and to teach them to be good citizens. Singapore teachers tell their pupils, "An educated person is someone who is responsible to himself, his family, and his friends . . . and to his community and his country." Schools teach good behavior, moral values, and a love for the nation of Singapore, as well as a wide range of academic subjects.

Pupils spend six years at elementary school, followed by five years at high school. Most continue their education at college. The government is especially keen for students to study subjects that will help them develop Singapore's economy, such as computing, engineering, and electronics.

Like Singapore's health-care service, education is run by a mixture of government-funded and private plans. Elementary schools are free, although parents have to pay for books and uniforms. High schools and colleges charge fees, although there are grants and scholarships to help pupils from poorer families.

The education system is very competitive. Parents and teachers encourage pupils to study hard and achieve high marks. Students are placed in classes according to ability, and the most able students are taught extra subjects that help them get into college and qualify for interesting, well-paying careers. All schools and colleges are open to all students regardless of their wealth, religion, or ethnic background.

Arts, Entertainment, and Sports

Singapore has a rich heritage of artistic traditions. These include opera from China, temple dances from India, and puppet plays from Southeast Asia. Singapore has also kept links with Western culture, dating from British colonial times. Today, Western-style music—classical and pop—and Hollywood movies are very popular, along with movies made locally and in Hong Kong. At night many young Singaporeans go to dance and watch rock bands at discos and clubs.

Sports such as *silat* (see-LAHT), a Malay martial art in which contestants use their hands and feet to overbalance their opponent, and *sepak takraw* (see-PAHK tuh-KRAW), a game similar to volleyball, attract many spectators. People like to watch modern sports, especially soccer, badminton, and squash, in sports stadiums or on TV. They also go to watch horse races at the Singapore Turf Club racetrack.

Actors taking part in a Chinese opera at Singapore's Clarke Quay, a popular entertainment district where many performances are held outside.

SRI LANKA

Sʀɪ Lᴀɴᴋᴀ ɪѕ ᴀ ʟᴀʀɢᴇ ɪѕʟᴀɴᴅ ɪɴ ᴛʜᴇ Iɴᴅɪᴀɴ Oᴄᴇᴀɴ, lying just south of the Indian subcontinent and separated from it by a narrow strait approximately 30 miles (50 kilometers) wide.

Much of Sri Lanka is made up of flat or gently rolling plains. In the south-central part of the island is a principal mountain mass, called a massif. The highest point of the massif is 8,282 feet (2,524 meters) at Pidurutalagala Mountain. The coastal belt is, on average, less than 330 feet (100 meters) above sea level.

The vegetation in the low-lying and wet southwest is lush, with dense tropical rain forests. The north is much drier, with savannah vegetation. Since ancient times, large parts of the island have appeared green and fertile, thanks to the Sri Lankans' understanding of irrigation. Thousands of artificial lakes, reservoirs, and ponds are dotted across the island.

Sigiriya Rock rises dramatically from the surroundings. An ancient fortress, palace, and monastery, it also has one of the world's oldest and most beautiful gardens.

Early History

The first known written references to Sri Lanka (SHREE LAHN-kah) appear in the Indian epic poem, the *Ramayana* (rah-muh-YAH-nuh). It tells how Sita was kidnapped and carried to the island kingdom of Lanka. In the sixth century B.C.E., Sinhalese (sihn-hah-LEES) people, probably from northern India, first came to settle in Sri Lanka. It seems likely that they conquered the island's earlier inhabitants, the

---

CLIMATE

Sri Lanka has a tropical climate, and on most parts of the island it is warm throughout the year. The southwest monsoon normally brings rain between May and September. During this time most rain falls in the south and west of the island and in the central highlands. The northeast monsoon brings rain, mostly to the north and east, between December and March.

	Colombo	Jaffna
Average January temperature:	79°F (26°C)	77°F (25°C)
Average July temperature:	81°F (27°C)	83°F (28°C)
Average annual precipitation:	88 in. (224 cm)	49 in. (124 cm)

FACTS AND FIGURES

Official name: *Democratic Socialist Republic of Sri Lanka*

Status: *Independent state*

Capital: *Colombo*

Major towns: *Galle, Jaffna, Kandy*

Area: *25,332 square miles (65,610 square kilometers)*

Population: *19,750,000*

Population density: *780 per square mile (301 per square kilometer)*

Peoples: *74 percent Sinhalese; 18 percent Tamil; 7 percent Muslim Moors; one percent others, including Burgher, Malay, and Vedda*

Official languages: *Sinhala, Tamil*

Currency: *Sri Lankan rupee*

National day: *Independence Day (February 4)*

Country's name: *Translates as "venerable place." Lanka is the ancient Sinhalese name, while Sri was added more recently.*

---

aboriginal ancestors of the Vedda (VEH-dah) peoples. There is little evidence on when the first Tamils (TAH-meels), Dravidian people from southern India, came to Sri Lanka, but it was probably also at least two thousand years ago.

The Sinhalese settled and began to grow crops in the dry, northern region. They developed a highly advanced system of irrigation, allowing large areas of land to be cultivated. Their populations grew, and two important centers of Sinhalese civilization arose, the city of Anuradhapura (ahn-yoo-rah-dah-POO-rah), and, later, Polonnaruwa (poe-loe-nah-ROO-wah).

Buddhism was introduced to the island from India in the third century B.C.E. and soon became established as the religion of Sinhalese monarchs and their people. The religion came to play a vital part in the political and cultural development of Sri

---

Time line:	Sinhalese people first settle on Sri Lanka	Rise of Anuradhapura; Buddhism introduced	Tamil-led Chola Empire conquers Anuradhapura	Arab traders arrive on island; new Sinhalese kingdom emerges
	500s B.C.E.	**200s B.C.E.**	**early 11th century C.E.**	**1100s**

511

Lanka. Buddhist art and architecture flourished, monasteries were built, and monks began to spread the teachings of the Buddha. Sri Lanka remained a stronghold of Buddhism, while on the Indian subcontinent it was largely replaced by Hinduism.

The Sinhalese kingdoms, centered on Anuradhapura and Polonnaruwa, lasted for over a thousand years, but they were often threatened—and at times briefly conquered—by more powerful neighbors in Hindu southern India. The Tamil-led Chola (CHOE-luh) Empire conquered Anuradhapura in the early eleventh century C.E. and ruled the kingdom as one

> ## *The* Mahavamsa
>
> *The* Mahavamsa *(mah-hah-VAHM-suh), or Great Chronicle, was composed by Buddhist monks in the sixth century* C.E. *It was written in verse, in Pali (PAH-lee), the language of Theravada Buddhism. Part history and part legend, it tells of the rise and fall of early Sinhalese Buddhist kingdoms. The hero of the* Mahavamsa *is Prince Vijaya, claimed by the Sinhalese as the founding father of their people. According to legend, Vijaya was the grandson of a north Indian princess, and Sinha, a lion. The Sinhalese call themselves "Sons of the Lion."*

A bronze statue showing a seated Buddha teaching his followers. This statue was made in the sixth century, during the time of the Anuradhapura kingdom.

of its provinces. When the Chola Empire began to decline in the twelfth century, a new Sinhalese kingdom emerged, with its capital at Polonnaruwa. Under the rule of Parakramabahu I, Sri Lanka's most revered king, the city became famous throughout Asia for its beauty and magnificence.

By the thirteenth century, however, the kingdom was in decline and the ensuing power struggles led to nearly two hundred years of political instability. During this time, the Tamil and Sinhalese communities became increasingly separate from one another. The Tamils established their own kingdom of Jaffna (JAHF-nuh) in the north. The Sinhalese center of power was at Kotte (KOE-teh) in the southwest, then later in the more inaccessible central highlands around Kandy (KAN-dee).

Portuguese traders take control of the spice trade	Dutch expel Portuguese from the island	Sri Lanka becomes first crown colony of British Empire	British rule whole island	Sri Lanka becomes fully independent
1400s	**mid–17th century**	**1796**	**1815**	**1948**

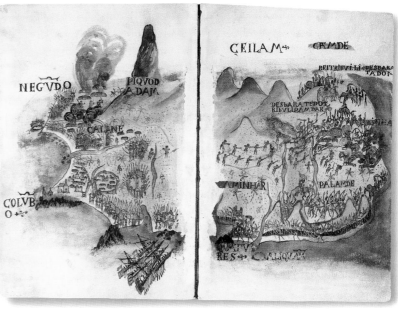

Taken from a book published in 1565, these maps indicate battle scenes between the Portuguese and the Sinhalese, showing how the Portuguese began to conquer coastal Sri Lanka.

An Island Trading Post

The geographical position of Sri Lanka in the Indian Ocean placed it at the heart of maritime trade routes between the East and West. Arab traders arrived in the twelfth century, followed in the fifteenth century by the Portuguese, who soon took control of the spice trade and conquered most of coastal Sri Lanka, converting many local peoples to Christianity. By the mid-seventeenth century, the Portuguese had been expelled by the more powerful Dutch, who allied themselves with the highland kingdom of Kandy.

British Colonial Rule

In 1796 the British took the important harbor of Trincomalee (trihn-COE-muh-lee) and expelled the Dutch. Sri Lanka became the first crown colony of the British Empire, and by 1815 the whole island was under British rule.

During this time of British rule, Sri Lanka was transformed. Large plantations were developed for growing cash crops such as coffee, cinnamon, tea, and rubber. Networks of roads and railroads were constructed to carry plantation crops to the coast. A shortage of cheap labor encouraged the British to bring in large numbers of Tamil workers from southern India.

The economic development of Sri Lanka brought social as well as economic change. A new Western-educated pro-British elite emerged. Political associations were formed and began to demand a say in government. By 1931 the British had granted internal autonomy and a one-person, one-vote system for the island. Full independence came in 1948.

Independence and After

The road to independence in Sri Lanka was peaceful, but the changes introduced by the British sowed the seeds of the conflict to come. The economy, which depended on agriculture, above all plantation crops, was vulnerable to fluctuating world prices. The population was expanding rapidly, leading to unemployment and competition for jobs. Government was dominated by the English-speaking elite. The rise of Sinhalese nationalism resulted in a "Sinhala

Rise of Sinhalese nationalism; Solomon Bandaranaike elected prime minister	Sirimavo Bandaranaike becomes prime minister	Sri Lanka moves away from socialist policies; tensions in main Tamil areas increase and Tamil Tigers formed
1950s	**1960**	**1970s**

Prime Minister Sirimavo Bandaranaike addresses a large crowd during election campaigns in March 1965. At the time, she was the world's only female prime minister.

(sihn-HA-lah) only" policy, in which Sinhala became the official language of the island.

In 1959 the prime minister, Solomon Bandaranaike, was assassinated by a Buddhist extremist. His widow, Sirimavo Bandaranaike became prime minister in 1960, and again in 1970. During this time, Sri Lankan governments pursued socialist policies, achieving virtual self-sufficiency in food, but leading to economic decline. By the late 1970s, a change of government saw the introduction of liberal economic policies and development aid from the West.

The dominance of the Sinhalese meant that the Tamils felt increasingly discriminated against, in language, religion, and political and economic power. More radical Tamils began to campaign for an independent state. In the 1980s this

discontent erupted into a full-scale guerrilla war in the north of the island, led by the Liberation Tigers of Tamil Eelam (LTTE), who became known as the Tamil Tigers. The ensuing conflict saw considerable violence on both sides, political assassinations, and terrorist bombing campaigns, especially in Colombo (coe-LOEM-boe).

After nearly twenty years of war, the government and the rebels finally agreed to a cease-fire early in 2002 and reached political agreement later that year. The Tamils have now agreed to regional autonomy rather than a separate state. At the end of 200 3 the fragile peace was still holding.

More than sixty thousand Sri Lankans died in the war, and one million have been displaced as a result. Many thousands of Tamils have fled the island. The conflict has also held back economic growth, discouraging investment and tourism.

People and Languages

The majority of Sri Lankans are Sinhalese, making up about three-fourths of the island's population. They probably migrated to Sri Lanka from northern India about 2,500 years ago. They speak Sinhala, an Indo-European language. Almost all Sinhalese are Buddhists.

The second largest ethnic group are the Tamils, who make up about 18 percent of the population. They are divided into the

Radical Tamils campaign for independent state; full-scale guerrilla war erupts on north of island, led by Tamil Tigers	Government and rebels agree to cease-fire; peace talks begin	President Kumaratunga in dispute with parliament over peace process; Tamils agree to regional autonomy
1980s	**2002**	**2003**

Sri Lankan Tamils, who have lived on the island for about two thousand years, and the Indian, or immigrant, Tamils, descended from the laborers brought in by the British in the nineteenth century to work on the tea plantations. Both groups are originally from southern India and speak Tamil, a Dravidian language. Most Tamils are Hindus, although a small number have converted to Christianity.

There are two other important minority groups living on the island, Muslims and Burghers (BUHR-guhrz). The Muslim community makes up about 7 percent of the population. Most of this community is known as Sri Lankan Moors and is descended from Arab traders who made the island their home about a thousand years ago. They speak Tamil, with Arabic influences. Burgher is used to describe any Sri Lankan who has European ancestry, although most Burghers are descended from Portuguese or Dutch colonialists.

The Wanniyala-Aetto

The Wanniyala-Aetto (meaning forest dwellers) are said to be the last surviving descendants of the island's aboriginal peoples. For thousands of years the Wanniyala-Aetto have lived as hunter-gatherers in Sri Lanka's forests. Traditionally they hunted wild animals with hand-carved bows and arrows, and gathered fruits and honey. They knew the forest plants and animals intimately and took from their surroundings only what they needed to survive.

Today the Vedda, or Wanniyala-Aetto, have lost much of their distinctive identity. Many have been absorbed into Sinhalese or Tamil communities, while others have been displaced as forest lands have been cleared for cultivation or irrigation. In the 1980s many of the remaining Wanniyala-Aetto were evicted from their forest homes when the Sri Lankan government created the Maduru River National Park in an attempt to protect the dwindling forest cover. In recent years a few Wanniyala-Aetto have been allowed to return to the forest, but their unique culture is in danger of disappearing forever.

Their numbers are much smaller today. Most speak English and are Christians. There are also a smaller number of Malays, who are also Muslims and who settled on Sri Lanka when it was ruled by the Dutch. They speak a Creole language, which is based on Malay.

Children have fun trying out their skills at stilt walking. At the Esala Peraheras Festival in Kandy, stilt walkers are a popular part of the spectacular parades that are held each year.

Men using age-old extracting methods to mine gems. Sri Lanka has twenty-five varieties of gemstone, of which the most precious is the blue sapphire.

Economy and Resources

Twenty years of conflict has inflicted a high cost on the Sri Lankan economy, yet it has continued to grow. Successive governments have invested in education and health care, as well as developing new industries. They have also encouraged large irrigation and hydroelectric projects to support the growth of both industry and agriculture.

The most important industry is textile manufacturing, which today makes up about 60 percent of the country's exports. Other important industries include the processing of food and other agricultural products, consumer goods, and telecommunications. Sri Lanka has also developed an offshore insurance and banking industry. Another vital sector of the economy is tourism. It has been badly affected by the years of conflict, but since the beginning of the cease-fire in 2002, has begun to pick up once more.

Agriculture remains the main livelihood for many Sri Lankans. The main food crop is rice, but large amounts of fruit and vegetables are also grown. Plantation crops are grown mostly for export. The most important crop is tea, but rubber,

The stilt fishermen of Ahangama, on the southern coast, are unique to Sri Lanka. This tradition has been handed down from father to son for many generations.

coconut, coffee, and spices such as cinnamon, cardamom, and pepper are also widely cultivated. Fishing has always been important to Sri Lanka, especially among Tamil communities in the northeast of the island. However, government restrictions on Tamil fishers in this area, and the disruption caused by the civil war, have led to a serious decline in fishing catches. In addition, most of the fish that is caught today is exported rather than used for local consumption.

More than one million Sri Lankans work overseas, mostly in Middle Eastern countries, and the money that they save and send home—estimated to be more than $800 million in 1998—provides an invaluable boost to the economy.

Health and Education

Over the last thirty years, the Sri Lankan government has placed great emphasis on improving the health of its people. It provides state pensions and free health services through the state-run network of hospitals, clinics, and drug stores. The government also runs public health programs to provide health education and to combat infectious diseases such as malaria. Health facilities are better in the towns; in many rural areas there are few doctors, and people rely on village drugstores.

The average life expectancy in Sri Lanka is sixty-seven years for men and seventy-four years for women. However, an aging population is likely to present problems in the future, putting increased pressure on both health services and state pension provision.

Although Sri Lankans use Western medicine, many also rely on the traditional system of medicine known as *Ayurveda* (ie-yuhr-VAE-duh). This ancient system of Hindu medicine focuses on diet and lifestyle, and uses medicines made from herbs, plants, and minerals. There are several thousand Ayurvedic practitioners in Sri Lanka, and the government provides training and research facilities for those who wish to become Ayurvedic physicians.

Sri Lankans place great value on education, and in the years since independence they have achieved one of the highest literacy rates in Asia. It is estimated that more than 90 percent of the population can read and write.

Children attend elementary school for six years, starting when they are six years old, and then go on to high school. This lasts for five years and can be followed by an

Part of a reforestation program, schoolchildren take and plant tree seedlings, which they have grown themselves, to help restore the forests in the hills surrounding their village.

People stand around a public faucet in Panadura, just south of Colombo, taking their daily bath. Many families do not have piped water or a bathroom in their home.

additional two years. The main language of instruction is either Sinhala or Tamil. Schooling is provided free of charge. However, a minority attend private, fee-paying schools or religious schools such as those run by Buddhist, Muslim, and Christian organizations.

Although the enrollment rates in schools are high, so are the dropout rates, especially in rural and poor urban areas. Many rural schools are under-equipped and find it difficult to attract the better-qualified teachers who prefer to work in the towns. In recent years the government has introduced educational reforms, with the aim of providing modern learning materials and more teachers, especially in remote rural areas.

There are many opportunities for further education, ranging from the eight colleges, including the prestigious University of Colombo, to technical colleges, offering practical and vocational courses, and agricultural colleges.

Village Life

Nearly three out of four Sri Lankans live and work in villages. Daily life focuses around farming or, in many coastal areas, fishing.

A typical village community has clusters of family houses, usually with their own compound and garden for growing vegetables. Beyond the houses lie paddies, where rice is grown, fields of cash crops, fruit, and coconut trees. Large ponds or

reservoirs supply plentiful water to irrigate the crops, so that even in the dry areas of the island, the countryside looks lush and green for much of the year.

A focal point for the community is the village shrine or nearby temple, where people often stop to make offerings of flowers or food. Small village stores and regular village markets are the lifeblood of rural communities. People go to markets to sell what they have grown or made, to haggle over the price of products or household goods, and to meet and gossip with friends.

The family lies at the heart of everyday life. Responsibilities are clearly divided. Men are expected to provide for and protect the family, whether they are farmers, fishers, traders, or businessmen. Women look after the home, raise the children, and plant, weed, and take part in harvesting the crops.

From an early age children are expected to help their families. Boys learn to take care of domestic animals, such as cattle and goats, and to protect ripening crops from wild animals. Traditionally, boys learned their father's trade or craft so that they could work alongside him, and eventually take over his responsibilities. Today, many families hope that a good education will enable a son to find a well-paying job, even if this means he has to leave the village. Girls learn household chores, such as cooking and cleaning, and look after the young ones in the family. They also learn to sew and make everyday household items, such as mats or baskets. Education is important for girls too, although once they are married, a career takes second place to family and home.

Children and their parents also help in the wider village community, especially at times when everyone pulls together, such as planting and harvest time, and during religious festivals.

Village life provides a strong sense of belonging, but many families are very poor. They often have only small plots of land or may be landless, working the land of a wealthier landowner for meager wages. Family members may have to leave the village in search of work elsewhere. Although the government has made basic facilities such as clean, piped water and modern sanitation a priority for both poor urban and rural communities, there are large numbers of villages where families still draw their water from wells and do not have access to electricity.

Nuwara Eliya, in the highlands, was much loved by the British for its cooler climate. Here they built elegant colonial houses and laid out British-style gardens, such as the one seen here.

Sri Lankans frequently mix and match Western and traditional dress. Men may favor the traditional sarong—a length of cloth that is wrapped around the lower half of the body and secured at the waist—and loose shirt. They may also wear Western-style pants or jeans. Sri Lankan women, especially among the Tamil communities, often wear Indian-style saris or long skirts with blouses.

Living in Colombo

Colombo, with a population of over one million, is Sri Lanka's capital and its largest city. It is a sprawling city of great contrasts. The more well-off inhabitants live in elegant houses with large gardens and tree-lined avenues. One of the most fashionable and wealthy neighborhoods is Cinnamon Gardens. On the edges of the city are the shantytowns of the poor. Many Sri Lankans have been drawn to Colombo in search of work, and today nearly half of the city's population lives in slum housing. There is poverty, unemployment, crime, traffic congestion, and pollution, yet many Sri Lankans find Colombo a congenial place to live.

The Daily Diet

Rice, which is widely grown across the island, provides the staple dish for most meals in Sri Lanka. It is usually eaten with a variety of small side dishes of vegetables, fish, or meat. Cooks have a wonderful range of fresh spices and flavorings to choose from, including coconut milk, cinnamon, coriander, turmeric, and chili, and usually make their food hot and spicy. They also have a huge variety of vegetables and fruits, often homegrown.

Ingredients and dishes from Indian, Arab, Portuguese, Dutch, and Malay peoples, who have come to trade or to settle on the island, have influenced Sri Lanka's cuisine. One popular dish is *biryani* (bih-ree-YAH-nee), from northern Indian, which is made with delicately spiced rice, often mixed with meat, fruit, or nuts. Southern

Tea Leaves

Large tea plantations cover the lower slopes of Sri Lanka's southwestern highlands. Tea grows best on sloping land in a warm climate. It is harvested throughout the year. Only the buds and the two youngest leaves are picked. All harvesting is done by hand, and by women. They work with a basket slung across their backs, held in place with a headband.

Women, in their bright saris, spread out across the lush, rolling hills of the plantations. However, life for these women is harsh: they work very hard for low wages, and they and their families live in poor, overcrowded housing, largely isolated from life outside the confines of the plantation.

Indian vegetarian *thalis* (THAH-lihs), or meals, have several small dishes and relishes, all served on a large plate. A particular favorite is *sambol* (SAHM-boel), a spicy side dish with Malaysian origins, made from onion, dried fish, salt, and red-hot chilies. Unique to Sri Lanka are *hoppers* (HAW-puhrz), which are often eaten at breakfast or as a snack. They are similar to pancakes and can be eaten with savory accompaniments, such as eggs or curries, or with jelly or honey.

Tea is widely drunk across the island, and tea breaks, at work or at home, are an important part of the day. People drink mostly water with

In Bandarawela, a market town in the central highlands of Sri Lanka, customers wait their turn to buy freshly baked bread, pastries, and cakes from a mobile bakery.

their meals. Alcoholic beverages include beer and two beverages made from tapping palm trees: freshly made, slightly effervescent toddy, and *arak* (ah-RAHK), liquor made from fermented toddy.

Buddhism

For more than two thousand years, Buddhism has shaped much of Sri Lanka's history and culture. About 70 percent of Sri Lankans are Buddhists. They follow the Theravada school of Buddhism, which is often regarded as the most orthodox and austere form of Buddhism.

Sri Lanka has several thousand Buddhist temples and monasteries. Lay Buddhists visit the monasteries regularly to listen to the teachings of the monks and to take care of their daily needs. Monks are greatly respected by lay Buddhists for their religious knowledge and understanding, and their frugal lifestyle.

Buddhism has always been characterized by its tolerance and kindness. However, in recent years, a less tolerant side of Buddhism has been seen in Sri Lanka, through the influence of some militant monks on politics and their attitudes toward Hinduism and the Tamil minority.

Other Religions

Hinduism is followed by most Tamils. There are also smaller, but significant, numbers of Muslims and Christians on the island.

The Hindu caste system exists in Sri Lanka, although it is generally less important than it is in India (see INDIA). It influences Tamil, and to a lesser extent Sinhalese, communities. There are

Buddhist monks visit the Rock Fortress at Sigiriya. Once a giant brick lion stood here, with stairs leading into its mouth. Today all that remains of the lion are its paws.

divisions between the long established Sri Lankan Tamils, many of whom claim to be descended from the higher castes, and the immigrant Tamils, who are often from lower or inferior castes.

Festivals

A religious festival is celebrated almost every month of the year in Sri Lanka. Muslim festivals follow the Islamic lunar calendar. Buddhist and Hindu festivals follow a lunar and solar calendar, so they fall on different days each year. The day of the full moon each month is seen as having special religious significance for Buddhists because they believe that the Buddha's birthday, enlightenment, and death all took place on the same day in different years—at the time of the full moon.

The most colorful of the Buddhist festivals are the *Esala Peraheras* (eh-SAH-luh peh-RAH-huh-rahz), held in July or August,

521

when the full moon of Esala appears. Peraheras, meaning "parades," are held in towns across the island and often last for six or seven days. The most spectacular of these is in the highland town of Kandy. Processions of elephants, dancers, musicians, and other performers weave their way through the town's streets. The elephants are draped in rich brocaded materials, embroidered in gold and silver thread. The most magnificent of all the elephants is known as the *Maligawa Tusker* (mah-lee-GAH-wah TUHS-kuhr), and on the penultimate day of the Perahera, he is honored with carrying the casket that holds a replica of the Buddha's Sacred Tooth.

Other important festivals are *Vesak* (VEH-sahk), the holiest day in the Buddhist calendar that honors the birth, enlightenment, and death of the Buddha, and *Poson* (POE-sawn), which celebrates the arrival of Buddhism in Sri Lanka.

A much-loved Hindu festival, especially among Tamil farming communities, is the harvest festival of *Thai Pongal* (TIE pawn-GAHL). It is held in mid-January, at the time when the rice is harvested. The celebrations usually last three or four days and begin with the boiling of the first grains of harvested rice with milk and honey. This sweet pudding is first offered to the Sun God, Suriyapakaran (soo-ree-yah-pah-kuh-RAHN), and then eaten at family feasts. Farmers also honor their cattle at this time, for the work they do in plowing the field and giving milk. Cows are bathed and garlanded with beads, flowers, and colored powder. This is a joyous time, when families spring-clean and decorate their homes, dress in their finest clothes, and cook and share special festival foods.

Tamil communities also celebrate the Hindu festival of lights, known in Sri Lanka as *Deepavali* (dee-puh-VAH-lee), in late October or early November.

The main festival for Muslims is *Eid ul-Fitr* (EED uhl-FEET-ruh), which takes place at the end of the monthlong fast of Ramadan. *Eid ul-Adha* (EED uhl-AHD-hah) is another important Muslim festival, known as the "feast of sacrifice." The island's Christian communities celebrate the important festivals of Easter and Christmas.

The Buddha's Sacred Tooth

The sacred tooth of the Buddha is probably the most important holy relic in the Buddhist religion. The Temple of the Tooth, in Kandy, where the relic is kept, is a site of pilgrimage for many thousands of Buddhists each year.

The relic is believed to have been smuggled out of India in the fourth century by Princess Hemamali from Orissa. She hid the tooth in her hair so that no one could get to it. Over the centuries the tooth was moved several times to keep it safe, before it ended up in Kandy. The tooth relic is kept in a shrine room, inside a golden casket.

Art and Architecture

Much of the artistic expression of Sri Lanka reflects the central place of Buddhism on the island. For more than two thousand years, Sri Lankan artists and craftspeople have made works that reflect devotion to the Buddha, yet also showing a distinctive Sri Lankan style. These crafts flowered when the ancient cities of Anuradhapura and Polonnaruwa were at their height. Today, the fine temples and palaces are being reclaimed from the rain forest, through painstaking excavation and study.

traced back over two thousand years. Most of the writing is religious in nature. Buddhist monks recorded the *Mahavamsa* and the *Jataka* (jah-TAH-kah), stories from the Buddha's life, which are still used today in Buddhist teachings.

Secular literature began to emerge about a hundred years ago. One of the leading writers of the twentieth century was Martin Wickremasinghe (1895–1976), who collected and wrote many works on Sri Lankan folklore. Today, well-known novelists include Sri Lankan-born Romesh Gunesekera and Michael Ondaatje, who both now live in the West, and the famous British-born science-fiction writer, Arthur C. Clarke, who has lived in Sri Lanka for nearly fifty years.

Ambalangoda is home to the ritual masked dance called kolam. *Today the dance has almost died out, but craftspeople still make these devil-masks, mostly for the tourist industry.*

The architectural structures that are most evident across the island are the ancient *dagobas* (DAH-goe-bahs), mound-shaped monuments that are a symbolic representation of the Buddhist world. They may contain Buddhist relics or treasures and are places of pilgrimage. The work of sculptors and painters often shows symbols or images of the Buddha. He is seen in different poses—sitting, standing, or lying. Around the ninth century, artists began to carve giant statues of the Buddha, hewn from the surrounding rock.

Literature

Sri Lankans have always had a love of storytelling. The storytellers of long ago often wove together fact and fiction to tell tales of ancient peoples and gods, lost kingdoms, and warring rulers.

The Sinhala and Tamil languages both have strong literary traditions that can be

Cricket: The National Sport

Team and racquet sports such as soccer, volleyball, and tennis are popular in Sri Lanka, but cricket is the national obsession. When important matches are being played, radio commentaries are broadcast loudly in town and village streets, and fans huddle around any available television to watch the game.

There are major cricket stadiums in Colombo, Kandy, and Galle. Sri Lanka has one of the leading cricket teams in the world and hosts matches against England, Australia, India, and Pakistan. Aspiring cricketers, especially young boys, will make a cricket pitch to play on wherever they can, be it by the roadside or in a village forest clearing.

Glossary

abaca a large plant related to the banana.

agribusiness the businesses and operations that are associated with farming.

animism the belief that things in nature, such as trees, mountains, and the sky, have souls or consciousness.

archaeology the scientific study of ancient cultures through the examination of their material remains, such as fossil relics, monuments, and tools.

archipelago a group or chain of islands; a wide stretch of water with many scattered islands.

asbestos any of several heat-resistant minerals used in the past to make fireproof insulation materials until it was discovered to be the cause of certain cancers.

asphalt a black substance used to make pavements.

causeway a raised path or road over a marsh or water.

cholera a serious and often fatal disease caused by the consumption of infected food or water.

coalition a temporary union among two or more groups.

cockfight an organized fight between two roosters in which the roosters usually wear metal spurs and are pitted against each other.

colony a country or area that is ruled by another country.

communist: a believer in communism, a theory that suggests that all property belongs to the community and that work should be organized for the common good.

cuttlefish a mollusk that lives on the ocean floor and has ten arms, a flat body, and an internal shell.

diabetes an illness in which a person has too much sugar in their blood.

diphtheria an infectious disease caused by a bacterium that attacks the membranes of the throat, releasing a toxin that damages the nervous system and the heart.

expatriate somebody who has left their homeland to live or work in another country.

guerrilla a member of an irregular fighting force whose tactics include ambushes, surprise attacks, and sabotage rather than intense, close battles with the enemy.

gypsum a colorless or white mineral used to make cement and chalk.

hub the most important or active part of a place.

hunter-gatherer somebody who lives by no other means than hunting and gathering.

immunization treatment (as with a vaccine) to produce immunity to a disease.

incense a spicy substance that is burned to create a sweet smell, especially during religious services.

irrigate to supply land with water brought through pipes or ditches.

karaoke a form of entertainment where a machine plays the music of a prerecorded song while someone sings along.

limestone a soft rock made from the decayed remains of ancient animals. Limestone is used as a building stone and in cement and fertilizers.

mandate an official instruction from an authority.

mangosteen a tropical tree that has large edible fruit.

mangrove any of various tropical trees or shrubs that grow roots and form dense masses in salty marshes or shallow saltwater.

martial law the control of a civilian population by the military forces.

migrant somebody who moves from one place to another in search of work or economic opportunities.

missionary somebody sent to another country by a church to spread its faith or to do social and medical work.

monarch a king, queen, or other royal person who reigns over a country.

monsoon a wind in the Indian ocean and southern Asia that blows from the southwest from April to October and from the northeast from October to April.

nomadic describes people who do not have a permanent home but instead move from place to place, usually in search of pasture for their animals.

oilpalm an African tree with fruit and seeds that provide the source of palm oil

peninsula a piece of land sticking out from the mainland into a sea or lake.

propaganda the spreading of ideas and information by a government or organization with the purpose of furthering or damaging a cause.

rambutan a Malaysian tree with edible red fruit.

rattan a climbing palm with long, tough stems.

separatist a person who favors separation from a religious group; a person who favors separation from a country, organization, or group of any kind.

settlement a place where people have settled and built homes.

soursop a tropical American tree with fragrant leaves and prickly fruit.

tripe the stomach lining of a ruminant, usually a pig, cow, sheep, or ox, which is cooked and eaten.

typhus a disease causing fever, severe headaches, and a rash that is spread by fleas and ticks and carried by rodents.

World War II a war that began in Europe in 1939 and spread to involve many other countries worldwide. It ended in 1945. The United Kingdom, France, the Soviet Union, the United States, Canada, Australia, New Zealand, and other European countries fought against Germany, Italy, and Japan.

Further Reading

Internet Sites

Look under Countries A to Z in the Atlapedia Online Web Site at
    http://www.atlapedia.com
Use the drop-down menu to select a country on the CIA World Factbook Web Site at
    http://www.odci.gov/cia/publications/factbook
Browse the Table of Contents in the Library of Congress Country Studies Web Site at
    http://lcweb2.loc.gov/frd/cs/cshome.html
Use the Country Locator Maps in the World Atlas Web Site at
    http://www.worldatlas.com/aatlas/world.htm
Look under the alphabetical country listing using the Infoplease Atlas at
    http://www.infoplease.com/countries.html
Use the drop-down menu to select a country using E-Conflict™ World Encyclopedia at
    http://www.emulateme.com
Look under the alphabetical country listing in the Yahooligans Around the World Directory at
    http://www.yahooligans.com/Around_the_World/Countries
Choose the part of the world you're interested in, then scroll down to choose the country using the
Geographia Web Site at
    http://www.geographia.com

Philippines

Gonzalez, Joaquin L. *The Philippines (Countries of the World)*. Milwaukee, WI: Gareth Stevens, 2001.
Gordon, Sharon. *Philippines*. Tarrytown, NY: Benchmark Books, 2003.
Gray, Shirley Wimbish. *The Philippines (A True Book)*. New York: Children's Press, 2003.
Lang, Thomas. *The Philippines*. Austin, TX: Raintree Steck-Vaughn, 2004.
Nickles, Greg. *Philippines: The Land*. New York: Crabtree Publishing, 2002.
Schemenauer, Elma. *The Philippines (Countries: Faces and Places)*. Chanhassen, MN: Child's World,
    1999.
Tope, Lily Rose R., and Detch P. Nonan-Mercado. *Philippines (Cultures of the World)*. Tarrytown, NY:
    Benchmark Books, 2002.
Wynaden, Jo; Joaquin Gonzalez; and Alan Wachtel. *Welcome to the Philippines (Welcome to My
    Country)*. Milwaukee, WI: Gareth Stevens, 2002.

Singapore

Baker, James Michael; Junia Marion Baker; and Scott Marsh. *Singapore (Countries of the World)*.
    Milwaukee, WI: Gareth Stevens, 2002.
Guile, Melanie. *Singapore*. Austin, TX: Raintree Steck-Vaughn, 2004.
Thomas, Matt. *Singapore (Countries: Faces and Places)*. Chanhassen, MN: Child's World, 2001.
Wee, Jesse. *Singapore (Major World Nations)*. Philadelphia, PA: Chelsea House Publishers, 2000.
Yong, Jui Lin; James Michael Baker; and Junia Marion Baker. *Welcome to Singapore (Welcome to My
    Country)*. Milwaukee, WI: Gareth Stevens, 2003.

Sri Lanka

Guruswamy, Krishnan. *Sri Lanka (Countries of the World)*. Milwaukee, WI: Gareth Stevens, 2002.
Kilgallon, Conor. *India and Sri Lanka*. Broomall, PA: Crest Publishers, 2002.

Index

Page numbers in *italic* indicate illustrations.

Page numbers in *italic* indicate illustrations.